more beautiful than you know

jennifer strickland

HARVEST HOUSE PUBLISHERS
EUGENE, OREGON

Cover by Left Coast Design, Portland, Oregon

Cover photo © Aleshyn_Andrei / Shutterstock

Backcover author photo by Natasha Brown Photography (www.natashabrownphoto.com).

Published in association with the literary agency of WordServe Literary Group, Ltd., www.wordserveliterary.com.

MORE BEAUTIFUL THAN YOU KNOW

Copyright © 2014 Jennifer Strickland Ministries, Inc.
Published by Harvest House Publishers
Eugene, Oregon 97408
www.harvesthousepublishers.com

Library of Congress Cataloging-in-Publication Data
    Strickland, Jennifer.
    More Beautiful Than You Know / Jennifer Strickland.
       pages cm
    Rev. ed. of: Beautiful lies. 2013.
    Includes bibliographical references.
    ISBN 978-0-7369-5632-1 (pbk.)
    ISBN 978-0-7369-5633-8 (eBook)
    1. Young women—Religious life. 2. Self-esteem in women—Religious aspects—Christianity.
    I. Title.
    BV4551.3.S768 2014
    248.8'43—dc23

2013043584

Printed in the United States of America

18 19 20 21 22 / VP-JH / 10 9 8 7 6 5 4 3 2

For Caris and April,
who have held these hands high.

Acknowledgments

My life story sculpted the message you hold in your hands. There are many precious people who had a hand in shaping this book. But first of all, God showed this message to me and I owe him the deepest gratitude. It transformed the way I saw myself and gave me the fuel to help young women see themselves with new eyes.

My husband, Shane, launched this message and continues to carry it by supporting my ministry of speaking and writing, and he never complains about the sacrifices he makes so I can be a voice to women. His parents, Larry and Linda, have devoted matchless time, energy, and love for this work to be born. Our children, Olivia, Zachary, and Samuel, have shaped this message by humbling me time and again and showing me the real meaning of beauty, which always begins at home. My parents, George and Jan, have weathered the storms that have resulted in the rainbow of these pages. And my dedicated team, Caris Leidner, April Cousens, Faith Stansky, Rachel Dee Turner, Jan Alexander, Megan Carter, and Alaina McLemore, have made this possible through prayer, perseverance, and lots of patience with me. Each person listed here should take pride and partnership in this message; it is just as much theirs as it is mine.

This book is for the *young* woman, and there are many who shaped it without knowing I was thinking about them. Thank you to Rashelle, Brittany, Britt, Caroline, Carissa, and Katie: As I wrote, I imagined you in the season I knew you best, when you were young and wrestling to find your place in the world.

Thank you to the women whose life experience I have drawn upon: Devi Titus, Tracy Levinson, Gayle Novak, Val Christner, Polly Wright, Kaylie Biggs, and Leah Springer. A huge round of applause also goes to Casey Norr, Erin Hamway, Liz Winter, and many more who sacrificed a lot of carpool time so this momma could write.

Finally, to the team at Harvest House, especially Bob Hawkins, Jr., Larae Weikert, and the lovely and brilliant Kathleen Kerr, as well as my faithful agent Greg Johnson: Thank you! You made my dream possible. You believed this message was for the mothers *and* the daughters. Through *More Beautiful Than You Know*, you have linked the generations. Hallelujah!

Contents

*The world's mirrors are ever changing,
but there is One who always tells the truth.*

1   The First Lie:

You Are What Man Thinks of You

I used to think a prince was the answer to everything,
but now I see even a prince needs a king.

In Search of a Prince

Each young woman is priceless in her unique way, whether she knows it or not. But right now they all look awkward: their dresses are too tight, too revealing, or too impractical; their makeup comes on too strong, their hair is too fancy and it makes me wish I could see them as they truly are. But at the moment they stand stiffly in rows, lined up as if in a pageant. They all wear their bravest faces. After all, they did choose to play this game. It's a game, strangely, that opens up their many hearts to one man, and to the millions who are watching.

As the Bachelor steps up to the plate, the women catch their breath in unison. The prince has arrived, and with him is a silver tray lined with red roses. Those to whom a rose is offered can stay and play the game to win his heart; those who do not receive a rose are out. As he presents the roses one by one to his selected contenders, the women begin to squirm. *Who's next? Will he pick me? Will I be last? Does he see my heart? Does he like her more? Does he adore me the way I adore him?*

When a woman receives a rose, she lights up: She is hereby declared beautiful. She is called lovable and accepted, and receives the applause. When a woman does not receive a rose, far more often than not, she departs in tears. She usually asks, *What is wrong with me? Why couldn't he see the beauty I have within?*

When I see these young women filled with potential, so hungry for that one man's affirmation, longing to receive the red rose that symbolizes their value, I can't help but see their humanity. Maybe I should laugh at them, at how silly this all is. But I know something that makes me care too much: Inside, we are the same.

Man is not your mirror, and if you make him one,
you may see a twisted version of yourself.

None of us need to stand in line to be told we are beautiful or lovable. Men are just men, not mirrors.

Maybe I'm wrecked for shows like this because they too closely resemble my experience as a model. One man (a photographer or client) and a roomful of girls, all vying for his nod—this was the entire setup of my career.

I want to jump through the TV screen and shake these young women and tell them, *His approval or disapproval says nothing about you! His desire for you, or lack thereof, doesn't make you worthy of love, or beautiful, or not! Your value is not wrapped up in him!*

But I can't jump through the TV screen. Instead, I'll tell you this truth: Man is not your mirror, and if you make him one, you may see a twisted vision of yourself.

❧

What is it about the fairy tales that makes them such a beautiful lie?

Before the princess meets the prince, she is just a common girl. Desperate, lonely, lost, and poor, she has little chance of escaping the ruthless world. But once the prince on the white horse gallops onto the scene, the view shifts.

In the prince, there is safety from the sorrow of her upbringing. In him, all her broken places are healed. He is the dawn of her dark night. He slays the enemy who hungered to rob her of her rightful place in the kingdom. Willing to face death for her, the prince becomes her salvation. When he descends on bended knee to ask her hand, she is rescued from a life of lonely torment. The moment she agrees to marriage, she transforms from a lowly girl dressed in rags to a beloved princess, gowned and crowned and destined for a wonderful life.

As a young woman, I believed the fairy tales. I wanted the whole story—the gown, the castle, the crown, the prince. But the few boys in my story kept taking my heart and wrenching it. One after another either abandoned and rejected me or failed me in some significant way. I could not heal the issues boys had with drugs, alcohol, school, money, or themselves. Although I tried to throw a rope even in the name of friendship, they had neither the hope nor the faith to grab it, and I certainly had no power to raise them.

My heart bore the mark of loss. Without realizing it, by my early twenties, I was disenchanted with the lies of the fairy tales and began to wander the world in hopes of finding something else to fill me. Like you, I craved unfailing love, but I decided I would conquer the world on my own. I would slay my own dragons. I would build my own castle. I would craft my own dreams.

For me, these wishes were potential realities, or so I thought. Because I had a professional modeling career at 17, I always seemed to have a plane ticket that would sweep me away to another world. It was an escape route the average princess might appreciate.

❀

My journey as a fashion model began when I was eight. I was an awkward, clumsy kid with long limbs. No matter how hard I tried, I wasn't any good at sports. I tried jazz, tap, gymnastics, and ballet, but disliked all of it. So in a hopeful attempt to help me with my coordination, my mother enrolled me in a charm class at a local modeling school. To both of our surprise, I liked it. That little school became a place where I could fit in. They even put me on their brochure. When I won "Miss Photogenic" in a pageant and was awarded "Most Potential Model" by my modeling teacher, I began to wonder if there was a future in it for me.

Throughout high school, my mother and I heard that if we really wanted to know if I could make it in the business, I needed to interview with Nina Blanchard, the queen of modeling agents on the West Coast.

So, at six feet tall and seventeen years old, long blonde locks falling to the middle of my back, I walked into Nina's office, wondering if I would be accepted or rejected. Her assistants decided I needed to meet the queen herself, and set me up with a Hollywood photo shoot and an appointment with Nina afterwards.

The photographer told me to bring a short tight black dress, black stockings, and black high heels. My mother and I bought the dress, and I went to the photographer's apartment for the photo shoot. Mom wanted to accompany me, but I was very headstrong and overruled her. My first Hollywood photo shoot took place alone—as did all of my future ones.

Something wretched happened to me on that first photo shoot; his opinion of me mattered too much. I had a deep need for approval and validation, and I looked to the guy on the other side of the camera to give that to me.

That evening, Mom and I went to Nina's office.

"Let me see her pictures," she said, wanting to view the proofs from the day's shoot. She looked up from her spectacles, her judicious eyes scanning me from top to bottom. This fiery red-haired woman possessed the power to either catapult my dreams to the moon or dash them against the rocks. Leaning forward, Nina spoke to my mother: "She has potential. We want her." With her veined hands and long red nails, she slid a contract across the desk.

Nina was part of my first beautiful lie: If a man or a woman thinks I'm worthy, I am. If he or she thinks I have potential, I do. If they want me, I'm wanted.

Nina sent me to the offices of the biggest companies. She got me in *Glamour, Seventeen, Cosmopolitan,* and *Vogue.* She introduced me to some of the biggest producers, photographers, and designers in the world. After I graduated from high school, Nina sent me to Europe. I lived in Hamburg, Germany, with a handful of other girls who were promised a future in modeling. Day by day, we would go from interview to interview, showing the clients our portfolios in hopes of getting bookings. I began working regularly, filling my portfolio with tear sheets (pages torn from magazines) which were proof to the American clients that I could handle the European market.

Humans can be become poisonous prisms for us,
distorting lenses that misshape our value.

At the end of the summer, I didn't want to return home; I wanted to go on to Milan, Paris, and New York for the runway season with the other girls. But I had a scholarship to college in the fall, so I chose to return to Los Angeles, knowing I could work in Hollywood while attending school. For the next four years, I maintained my scholarship and majored in broadcast journalism; deep down, I knew I could speak and write.

While in school, I appeared in music videos, catalogues, TV commercials, and clothing campaigns, but as soon as classes ended for summer I flew back to Europe. My friends all went home to rest with their families and do odd jobs, and I went to foreign nations where I fought for my place in the world of modeling.

Although I lived with other models, I spent most days alone. I'd go from streets to subway stations to buses to trams to hotels to office buildings to sets, touching up my makeup in between interviews, checking in with the agency, while stylists made me look like a different person every day.

At first the lifestyle seemed harmless. My parents, who knew very little about the sordid side of the business, were in great support of my modeling career. Everyone from home cheered me on. They all saw modeling as an opportunity to see the world and make money doing it. No one raised any red flags, questioning if it was wise for a young woman like me to travel the world alone. And no one seemed to be wary of the impact the men who ran the agencies might have on me.

The modeling industry sets young women up to be alone with men, all the time. Interviews are often in photographers' studios or apartments; and even on the set, sometimes a photographer will take a model to a place separate from the crew. Sometimes the men were respectful; other times, they were not at all. Sometimes they complimented the models; other times, insults spewed from their mouths.

I also hurt myself during those years. I opened myself up to drugs, alcohol, the partying lifestyle, and relationships that hurt me deeply in the end.

After college I went to Italy, convinced that the runway would open the door to success. Prior to arriving I did everything I could to measure up to the standards of the European designers while losing the extra pounds of college weight: I tanned, fasted, sweat, dieted, ran, did yoga, ran some more, fasted some more, took vitamins and fat burners galore, straightened my hair, bought new clothes, worked out some more, packed my bags, and practiced my Italian.

But no matter how much you make over your outside, the heart is still scarred beneath the surface.

The Kings of Me

In Milan, I had almost immediate success. While the other models in my apartment were trudging along trying to get small jobs, the agents esteemed me from the beginning. Magazine moguls and the fashion elite were telling me I could become a "top model."

After the photo shoots, the men in the business often invited me out for dinner or dancing, which was customary for models. These men were typically twice my age or older, and I foolishly thought that because of their age, they would not take an interest in me romantically. Certainly that was the last thing on my mind. I simply wanted to experience the "beautiful life" promised me in Italy, and hoped these men would advance my career.

How stupid I was to believe that these older men would expect nothing in return. On several occasions I found myself either politely or forcefully having to let them know I was not interested in them physically.

One man in particular presented himself as a father figure to me, promising to "protect" and "watch over" me as my manager in Milan. He fed me fine Italian food and wine, offered to buy me pretty things, and began to promote my career. He appeared to only want what was best for me, so I quickly allowed him that fatherly role in my career. But of course the night came when he revealed that he wanted more.

When he came after me, I refused him. It was a miracle that I got away from him. But he still held the reins of my career and had a huge influence on my self-image. This experience left me feeling dirty, worthless, and sad. Never before I had I felt so far away from home, from my values and upbringing, and from the young, hopeful girl who started out with stars in her eyes. I became lost and dejected, lonely and afraid. Physically I no longer looked like the happy, bright girl in my pictures.

You are worthy of love. You are a daughter of the King, and no human being can dispose of that truth within you.

Over time I realized I was just a *thing* to all these men—a thing in a world of things, as disposable as a Barbie doll. To them, I was no one's daughter, no one's sister, no one's friend, and certainly no one's future wife. The word for model in French is *le mannequin*, and that's what we were to most of the men—mannequins upon which they could hang the clothes; mannequins they could position however they wanted; mannequins they could take apart and discard when a new model came to town. Plastic things to be bought, sold, traded, and disposed of when they were done with us.

When they lavished me with compliments I felt beautiful, but when they cursed me with insults I felt disposable. The men in the business began saying I was ugly and sad-looking. At one time, I was their little "discovery," their prized possession; and the next moment I was yesterday's news crumpled up in the trash.

I had been doing the runway for the king of fashion, Giorgio Armani, which was the pinnacle of my life as a model. But I starved myself for him; I had to be anorexic to succeed on the runway. When I became sick from not eating, my skin broke out in cystic pimples. Dark circles clouded my eyes and bruises marred my legs. I no longer looked like the porcelain-skinned girl in my portfolio.

Do you think the men invited me out for dinner and dancing then? Surely not! My "fatherly" manager shamed me for the flaws on my face and body. He dumped me as if I were just a plastic mannequin and not a human being in pain.

Soon afterward, I began to have wicked headaches and blurred eyesight. The acne began to take over my face—a death sentence for a model's career. As I tried to please Armani, my body withered to a dangerously skeletal state. There wasn't anything pretty about it.

Since everyone was telling me I was too thin, I tried to eat heartily for a week or two, even stuffing my face to gain weight. But when I showed up for the spring runway shows, Armani could feel the extra half inch around my waist. With a flick of his hand he immediately sent me off the stage. The stylist removed my clothes and left me standing in my underwear in the massive dressing room, wondering what had happened, until someone finally told me they were "finished" with me.

I went back to the agency, and the men there were clearly upset with me. My job was to make them money by looking perfect, so this didn't sit well. Armani cancelled me for the shows, and the rest of my jobs that month were cancelled too—one photographer even refused to pay me for a five-day job because he said I was anorexic, had acne, was insecure, and was so ugly he couldn't stand to take pictures of me.

My booker was infuriated. "You look sick!" he hollered at me. "You are as pale as mozzarella! You need to get some sun!" Then he turned toward a new, fresh-faced girl who had just come to town and started fawning her with the same attention he'd given me when I first arrived.

I had allowed these men to be my mirror, and in the reflection of that mirror all I saw was a twisted view of my value: I was only as good as they said I was. Only as worthy as their opinion of me. I was likable if they liked me, beautiful if they said so, ugly if they so declared.

❧

The sickness of making men my mirrors started young for me. As a teen, boys were my mirror. In high school and college, I handed a couple of boys my heart like magazine paper, and I walked away with a handful of shreds.

But something worse happened in my twenties, when I was looking for a father figure without even realizing it. I had a father at home—a good man—but he never knew about my fears, failures, and insecurities because we just didn't talk about them. Neither did my mother: She didn't ask; I didn't tell. So when those parental figures in the modeling industry approved of me, I felt secure. When they disapproved, I felt insecure. I looked to them for my value, so when they rejected me, saying I was no longer good enough, perfect enough, pretty enough, I began to see only what was wrong with me. The way they saw me became the way I saw myself.

We are messy miracles looking to a King.

Humans can become poisonous prisms for us, distorting lenses that misshape our value. When we give them power, they can completely change the way we see ourselves and the way we see the world.

Dumped

Ten years after I left the modeling business I began to speak publicly about my experience. At one particular event, there was a long line of girls waiting to talk to me afterward. I saw one girl in line who reminded me of myself at seventeen: tall with long, blonde curly hair and opalescent skin. She had big, bright Bambi eyes, a wiry frame, and an eager, almost hungry look on her face.

She was with her mother, and I was immediately concerned the girl was going to tell me she wanted to get into modeling. Although I am regularly confronted with modeling questions, I don't enjoy having this conversation. I always have to tell the girl and sometimes the mother something they don't want to hear.

On one hand, I either gingerly hint that the girl doesn't have the right bone structure or body or height to be a model and should pursue education and sports, which build healthy self-esteem. Or else I carefully tell them, "Yes, you do have the body and the look, but you are too precious to be treated like a piece of flesh. You should discover your gifts and talents and pursue them instead, because one day you won't be so pretty anymore and you'd better have something else to rely on! Plus, if you go into modeling, you will receive so much criticism or approval based on your outward appearance that you are going to become majorly messed up in the head." (I personally didn't live with any models who weren't.)

When the girl got to the front of the line and stood before me, she clasped her hands in front of her body as if to protect herself. She thanked me for my talk, and then her body began to tremble as she told me what she really waited in line to say: Just a few weeks ago her father told her she was worthless, ugly, and stupid and threw her in a dumpster.

I asked her to clarify: "Your father literally, physically picked you up and threw you into a dumpster?" Her big eyes filled with stinging tears and she shuddered as the tears began to spill. I could see her shattered heart, her wanting soul, her broken mind.

"Yes, he wrestled me down and I couldn't get away. He threw me into the dumpster…I was smothered in trash and I was trapped and I couldn't get out…"

Her body gave way and she quaked with heaving sobs; she could no longer speak. So I held her. I could feel my heart pressing against hers, speaking through her cries. "He was wrong about you, baby girl," I whispered in her ear. "He is sick and you can't believe him. You are precious and wonderful and God has dreams for you…"

And then, the inevitable: The mother said the daughter had had some opportunities to get into modeling, and what did I think of that? They could really use the money…

Now there's an idea! I thought. Let's take this little wounded deer and send her into the field to meet a bunch of wolves. Maybe we'll make some money! Let's take this desperate-for-daddy's-love girl and put her in front of a bunch of men her father's age, day after day, hour after hour, for them to evaluate her, accept her, reject her, try to have sex with her, try to get her topless or even naked in front of the camera! Yes, this is brilliant! This girl has a huge hole in her soul. Her father has not only told her she is ugly and worthless, but he has even hurled her into piles of rotting trash, where she has landed soiled and sobbing and beaten and bruised from the inside out. So maybe the men in the modeling industry can rebuild her self-esteem by taking pictures of her in bathing suits or fur coats and paying her thousands of dollars a day to smile and look pretty and act like she's not in pain at all. Maybe teaching her to wear a perfect mask is all the hope we have. Can someone please paint up her face and tell her she's pretty so she'll feel better?

Inwardly I weep for this. Inwardly, I rage.

How about some counseling? A good pastor? A youth group? An art class? Or best of all, long walks with a healthy, whole mother who can replace her father's lies with truth. Ideally, Mom can help her stand up straight again while Jesus brushes off all that debris. How about teaching her, *In God's eyes, that was a sin and no man will ever have the opportunity to trash you again, sweetheart. I'm going to make sure of it!*

Instead, the mother thinks the modeling industry could help.

I excused myself from the daughter, took the mother into a corner, and held her kindly yet firmly by the shoulders. I looked into her eyes and unequivocally said, "NO."

"There's such good money in it…I just thought it would give her opportunities…"

Mm-hmm, and there's great money in prostitution too. And that will give you plenty of opportunities.

What this girl needs—and what every daughter needs to know—is that she is worthy of love. She is a precious jewel. She is *not* worthless, and she is not defined by what man thinks of her. She is defined by God: a daughter of the King, and no human being can dispose of that truth within her.

Rescued

I hit my own personal rock bottom before I discovered this truth. After things went south for my modeling career in Milan, I moved to Munich, Germany. Everyone advised me to make as much money as I possibly could in the business before leaving it. Girls can make lots of money modeling for German catalogues, so off to Germany I went.

My roommate in Munich was a lingerie model who was as cold as the icy sidewalks I trudged up and down every day looking for work. She wouldn't share a blanket with me; a cup; a bowl; and certainly wouldn't sit at the table to eat with me, so night after night I sat at the dinner table alone. I oscillated from starving myself to binging, sometimes drinking myself to sleep, and would stay in my bed for long hours while voices ripped at my self-worth. Demonic forces blasted lie after lie through my mind: *I am ugly; I am worthless; no one wants me; no one loves me; there is no way out.* These thoughts whipped my mind into circles like a merry-go-round.

One night it got to be too much for me. In a moment of quiet, calculated desperation, I thought I wanted to die. But in my darkest hour I remembered my mother and those who loved me. I chose life in hopes that I could turn a corner in my soul.

The next morning, I was lying in bed when I heard a voice, clear as day, coming from the window.

"Jennifer, get up," it beckoned. I sat straight up and looked around but saw no one, so I lay back down. I didn't want to get up. It was so warm under the covers.

"Jennifer, get up," it said again.

This time I sat straight up; I stood up.

That day, I decided not to go to my auditions. Instead, I went to the park and stayed there all day. The Danube River runs through the English gardens in Munich like an ice blue ribbon weaving through an emerald landscape. There is a giant stone gazebo perched on a hilltop where people gather in the evenings to watch the sunset, play music, or have a picnic. I felt jealous of the friends. I envied the food they ate so freely. I envied their companionship and especially their laughter.

I chose a seat at the base of one of the pillars in the gazebo so I could hear the music. A man behind me was singing and strumming his guitar, his voice high and sweet. I turned to look at him and he reached down into an old cardboard box of books and handed me a New Testament.

The cover of it was sapphire blue and the words were engraved in gold. I took it in my hands. It was written in German.

He and his friends hardly spoke any English. There was a girl named Miriam who played the tambourine, a funny guy named Stephen, and the guitar player, Michael. They were so kind that when they realized I was alone in the park, they offered to walk me out.

Right when we were nearing the edge of the darkened wood, these strangers stopped to pray for me. It was the oddest thing. They asked if I would like to go to church with them that Friday night. I didn't feel that anyone on the continent cared about what happened to me, so I went.

In that church, people looked me in the eye. They didn't look at my body or measurements or skin or pictures. They saw who I was on the inside. I didn't understand a word of the German they spoke, but it didn't matter. They saw my heart and fed my soul's hunger. The third time I went to the church, a teenage girl named Naomi came bounding out from the back pews with a little book in her hands, barely able to contain her excitement.

"Jenny-fair! Jenny-fair! I have found you an English Bible!" she exclaimed, her face radiant.

The worn, thin pages felt good in my hands. I shoved it in my back pocket and took it home.

Back in my apartment at night, I grew curious about that little book. Somehow it wooed me only to itself. I began to thirst for its life-giving words; eventually I flushed my drugs down the toilet so I could focus only on it.

As I read, I fell in love with the way Jesus touched those our world doesn't want to touch. I loved the way he loved the weak, the broken, the confused. I felt like I'd been waiting my whole life to meet him. I kept that little book in my back pocket and read it on trains, waiting for interviews, and at home at night. Instead of drugs and alcohol, the Word became food to me. But it doesn't light you up and burn you out like drugs do; it lights you up and *keeps* lighting you up.

By candlelight I read most of the book of Matthew and packed my backpack for a weekend away from cameras and people. I took a train to Mount Zugspitze, the highest mountain in Germany, and stayed at a little bed and breakfast to finish reading the Gospels. In my rented room, I sat at a tiny desk and looked out the window at the falling snow. Snuggled in a blanket wrapped from my shoulders to my toes, I read the story of the end of Jesus's life.

In the pages of that little book, I discovered a man who loves me despite the ways I fall short of others' expectations. I discovered a man who accepts me as I am. A man who offers me freedom from the slavery of people's opinions. I discovered a prince on a white horse and a king who will never leave me.

Only God's love can raise a dead girl to life.

High on the mountain, on a pure white blanket of snow, I lay down on the ground and opened up my heart to him. I knew nothing about

Scripture or theology or denominations or church. I just knew I'd found the one my soul loves, and he was my only hope. There in the snow, I opened up the window of my heart and asked him to come in and make me new.

After fifteen years in the modeling industry, I packed my bags and left. I didn't need to explain to anyone why I was leaving. I walked away from an entire world that says: *You are what I say you are. You do what I say you do. And I am done with you when I'm done with you.*

It was my turn to speak, and by leaving, I said: *This is not beautiful to me, and I am going in search of what is.*

Prince Charming

I took the money I made modeling and went back to school to get my Master's degree in writing. I had always loved to write, and I was determined to use that gift to help girls see the illusion of beauty created by the media and point them toward a beauty and value that really lasts. For almost four years, I studied the Scriptures, wrote, and taught English. Then, I met my prince.

Crazy as it sounds, I realized it was him when we were riding horses on the sandy beaches of Mexico. My brother was bringing his girlfriend on a weekend getaway and asked if there was anyone I wanted to invite. I had been on one date with Shane, and scared to death, I told my brother to invite him.

Shane ran out to get new tires on his truck to make sure we would be safe. Driving all the way down to Mexico, he played DJ, and by the time we arrived I had been laughing and smiling for a few hours so I knew I made the right choice. Except for one thing: When we got there, he pitched a tent and I realized I was in a very awkward position—there was no way a good Christian girl like me was going to get in a tent with that boy! So instead, we walked on the beach and talked clear till sunrise, made breakfast at camp without a wink of sleep, and spent the next day riding four-wheelers. Later that afternoon, we went horseback riding.

On this particular beach, the horses for rent were tired, slow, and worn. Their speckled and spotted coats were heaving and sweating, carrying unsatisfied tourists on their backs. As Shane and I sat on the beach watching this pathetic display, we leaned in and whispered to each other, "I wonder if we could get those horses to run."

When it was our turn, we mounted and kicked them into action. Like lightning, they bolted.

When the crowd on the beach saw those mangy horses coming at them in full gallop, they ducked for cover. With a smile and a nod, Shane pointed to the islands and we took off for the horizon. Water sprayed from descending hooves in crystal beads and the wind lifted us under its wings. Riding on a speckled white stallion, Shane was thinking, *I'm a cowboy. I know how to ride a horse, and there is no way this California girl is going to keep up with me.* But when he turned his head to see how far he'd left me in the dust, I was right there beside him.

The sun flashed its golden light on his cheek. I saw the reflection on his face and my heart skipped. I knew I'd found my prince.

I e-mailed my best friend when I got back. "I met a guy named Shane. We rode horses on the beach and I'm going to marry him!"

"Simmer down," she wrote back. "We're not living on a soap opera!"

"Oh yes we are!" I responded. I had no intention of simmering down and neither did he. When we got back from Mexico, he asked when he could see me again. I suggested the following Friday. He responded, "I mean, when can I see you *tomorrow*?" We saw each other every day thereafter.

Fourteen years later, he still calls me his bride.

None of this would be possible without Christ, who reached into the darkest corner of my heart and offered me a whole new life. He did an even greater work redeeming Shane. We are just two messy miracles, looking to a King.

When we try to make a guy our rock, foundation, or anchor, we find ourselves blown and tossed by the storms. As wonderful as a prince can be, he needs a rock too. Men are made in the image of God but they are as hard-pressed for answers as we are sometimes. No human is without flaw; no human is a mirror reflection of us. This job is God's alone.

We must remember that God came as a man, and only his love can raise a dead girl to life.

You Are a Beloved Daughter

Daughter, your faith has healed you.

Mark 5:34

The Mirror of Man

In the fairy tales, the love of the prince magically transforms the girl's life. But most of the Disney princesses were already of royal descent before they ever met the guy on the white horse. Snow White, a fatherless orphan ruled by a wicked stepmother, was already a princess before she met the prince. Sleeping Beauty was too. Jasmine was a motherless princess rebelling against her kingly father, as were Ariel and Pocahontas. Cinderella was a much-loved daughter, but both her parents were deceased and she was stuck with a wretch of a stepmom. Belle was a beloved daughter, and it was her love for her father that led to her prince. They were all loved and cherished. They each possessed real beauty and a great destiny before the prince swept them away.

But the fairy tales lead us to believe that the prince possesses the power to declare them princesses; in *him* is the promise that all things will turn out well. Such is not the case with real princesses; their inheritance is sure, and it comes not from the prince, but from the bloodline of the king.

When I was writing *Girl Perfect,* my first book based on my experiences as a model, I reviewed heaps of diaries from my teen years in hopes that I would discover how I felt getting a contract at seventeen and what my dreams were when I went off to Europe. But there was barely a mention of modeling in those diaries. Page after page, book after book, it went the same way: "Luke asked me to the dance! I'm so excited! I think he really likes me!" Then…"I am so mad at Luke. He didn't even look at me after the game. He was talking to Carla, AGAIN! She is so pretty. I know he likes her more than me." Then…"I think I really like Danny now. He was looking at me in the quad during lunch. I'm hoping he's going to ask me to the prom!!!! I would be so happy!"…And…"I can't believe Danny asked Julia to prom! I am so mad! I feel like, *What's wrong with me? Am I not pretty enough? What is it?* I am crushed!!!"

And so the roller-coaster ride continued, on and on through college and then on over to Europe, until I was so tired of riding it I could barely stand.

God is our hiding place from the storm and the rain.

For many of us, loss of some sort drives us to search high and low for a love we already possess; brokenness within us makes us think a man can fix it; and nearly all of us believe the lie that our future begins the day we wear the white gown and those precious wedding day slippers, and dance in our prince's arms with the spotlight flooding upon us.

In many ways, marriage is a huge beginning for us. But marrying our personal princes in no way declares us any more lovable, beautiful, and destined for hope and a future than we are before the day we meet him. Just ask a woman of divorce, or one who suffered an unloving marriage. Just ask one whose husband has died, or lied; just ask a woman who knew her true value long before her wedding day. You will find out a man doesn't give us value; our value is ours, and ours alone.

When we turn away from the mirror of man and look instead into the mirror of God, the Bible, we discover man is a mist, here one day and gone the next (James 4:14). In the Psalms, David even asks the question, "What are human beings that you care for them, mere mortals that you think of them? They are like a breath; their days are like a fleeting shadow" (Psalm 144:3-4). Isaiah writes, "All people are like grass, and all their faithfulness is like the flowers of the field. The grass withers and the flowers fall, because the breath of the LORD blows on them" (Isaiah 40:6-7). God can literally blow his breath on a man, and that man can fall down dead.

God on the other hand, is forever. And he does not change or shift like a shadow. He even takes care to remind us he is *not* man. "God is not man, one given to lies, and not a son of man changing his mind. Does he speak and not do what he says? Does he promise and not come through?" (Numbers 23:19 MSG).

Guys can make promises and not keep them. They can make mistakes. They can disappoint us. They can change their minds, leave us, and choose another. And even the greatest, most faithful men die.

God, on the other hand, never leaves us. Never disappoints. Never changes his mind about us. Never betrays. Never falls. He is our ally, our stronghold, our deliverer, our fortress, our high tower, our refuge, our shelter and shade from the heat of the day, our hiding place from the storm and the rain (Psalm 144:1-2; Isaiah 4:6).

People were never designed to be all of this for us. Boys were not made to be your rock, your refuge, your hiding place. At times they can feel like this to us, but they cannot sustain that role. Boys and men may be good reflections of a loving God, but they are not the source of our security.

God is no dimly lit mirror; he is a perfect reflection.

The natural longing for approval from men becomes unhealthy when we expect a guy to be our security, the one in whom we put our faith. When he can't offer that, we feel sorely disappointed. He becomes not only a distorted mirror but a twisted lens through which we see ourselves. In sum, we've given him far too much power.

Yet when we turn our heads and look up to the One who originally fathered us, the King who holds our inheritance in his hands, we see clearly. God is no dimly lit mirror; he is a perfect reflection. When we look to him for our value, we are more able to love, because our faces become reflections of the Father's heart towards the men in our lives, and this is beautiful to any man. There is nothing more attractive to a man than a woman who already knows who she is; a woman whose confidence, joy, and faith is unshakable because it's founded in an unshakable God.

The Mirror of God

I get letters all the time from girls who have been abused, rejected, belittled, molested, abandoned, or let down, and the pain they feel is real. Wounds from man can be agonizing. On my own level, I understand this heartache.

Pain inflicted by man can define us if we let it. We can choose to walk as broken victims our whole lives. We can allow the pain of absent or abusive fathers to direct the road ahead, ending up in search of another father who in turn fails or forsakes us. We can try to fill the void of *daddy* with boys who don't know how to handle our hearts. And we can allow man's cruel words to plant themselves in our souls and grow vines that suck the vibrancy right out of us.

On the flip side, we can be addicted to praise from men, riding their compliments and applause like a magic carpet. Then, when the winds of praise grow still, we can suddenly fall crashing from the sky.

I recently spoke at an event where I said how hurtful it can be if the men in one's own home degrade a girl—especially her father. The moment I said it, a girl in the center of the audience got up and ran out of the room, crying. Afterward, I spoke with her. The girl was pursuing modeling, and her father told her she would never be perfect enough for the camera.

But here's the real blow: He abandoned their family, and the last words he said to her were, "You are such a disappointment." That word—*disappointment*—had rooted deep, and this girl was about to live her whole life focused on his careless curse.

I looked into her eyes and told her that he was wrong about her. He was the disappointment, not her. He was the one who left his family, not her. She was darling and lovable and had all the attributes of a princess—hope, dreams, and a future.

This girl was a fighter—literally, a boxer.

"When you're in the ring," I asked her, "what do you do when someone knocks you down? Do you stay down?"

Her eyes teared up. "No, I get up."

"Then get up and put on your gloves and decide he was wrong about you," I told her.

Man can say things that are wrong. His words can be like swords that thrust into the most tender areas of our hearts. Man's insults can wound the soul. But it's up to us to decide if we are going to let him define us and our futures…or God.

There is nothing more attractive than a woman whose confidence, joy, and faith is unshakable because it's founded in an unshakable God.

There are men in my life whom I hold in the utmost regard, who have shaped me in very positive ways, and who I look to for guidance and direction. I have just learned, and these men would agree, that God is the only secure foundation on which to build a life.

Surround yourself with people who build you up and do not tear you down. Even better, choose men who point you to the Father for your true value.

The Father Speaks

My dear one, do not form your image of me from man. Some men reflect my image well; they mirror forgiveness, grace, patience, kindness, and a love that protects and endures. But some men try to create a new definition of me. In the mirror of that definition, you may be confused about who I am. You may feel that I am inaccessible, angry, or distant. You may feel that you are not good enough for my approval, or that you'll never live out the dreams of your heart.

I want you to redefine who I am by looking into the mirror of my Word. I am your provider, your security, your canopy, and I hold a banner over you that says, "Loved."

As your heavenly father, I watch over all your comings and goings. I see every failure, every hurt, every victory, every valley and mountain you'll climb, and if a storm tears your precious heart, I see it and feel it. These are things your earthly father could never fully know.

You don't have to earn my approval. Before my Son Jesus ever performed a miracle, before he ever fed the thousands, before he taught a single parable, and long before he went to the cross, I spoke a word over him that I speak over you now: "This is my Son, whom I love. With him I am well pleased."

This is the life I want for you, daughter: to walk as one who knows she is beloved.

Look away from the mirror of man. Look at me! See your true reflection in the mirror of me.

❧

In my dealings with women and girls, I've found the most common wound people experience is from their fathers. Personally, I have seen how God can stand in the gap. When my earthly father wasn't present, my heavenly Father was; when my earthly father didn't understand me, my heavenly Father did; and where my earthly father fell short, my heavenly Father filled the areas of vacancy to overflowing.

I traveled this wild world by myself at a young age, and I came across many men who didn't care whose daughter I was. The pain led me to my heavenly Father. I needed his protection, guidance, and healing—all of which he offered me. Since then, the injuries from my broken road have been restored to me a hundredfold as my story has served as healing balm to others' shattered hearts.

Our personal experiences with men do not define our heavenly Father. God defines himself. And in the reflection of him, we see who we are and what we're worth.

The Princess Bride

A story in the Old Testament shows the Father's heart for his daughters. In Ezekiel 16, God uses the symbol of a helpless infant girl to paint a picture of his love for his people. He describes a baby girl who was completely unloved from the moment she was born. No one washed her when she came out of the womb or wrapped her in a blanket; instead, her demented parents threw her out into an open field. Naked and bare, the defenseless baby was kicking about in the rubble and bleeding. She was fighting for her life when God showed up.

"Then I passed by," the Father said, "and as you lay there in your blood I said to you, 'Live!'"

No matter where you are or where you've been, God sees. He sees how you have been taken care of or how you have been rejected. If you have been neglected or abused or abandoned, he sees it. If you have felt forsaken or despised or unloved, he knows it.

When God passes by, he says to you, "Live!" Don't curl up and die from the things man's done or not done for you or to you. What man may do to crush your spirit, God can restore and heal.

In the Ezekiel story, the Father's love makes the baby girl grow and develop. She becomes the most beautiful of jewels. Under his care, she matures into a lovely maiden with long hair and develops breasts. His protection and nurture feed her like water and the once-broken girl blossoms.

He continues to tell her powerful story: "Later I passed by, and when I looked at you and saw that you were old enough for love, I spread the corner of my garment over you and covered your naked body. I gave you my solemn oath and entered into a covenant with you…and you became mine." When the girl is old enough to experience the breadth of his love and purpose for her, he not only calls her daughter, but he weds her like a bride. He makes a promise to her that she will be his forever, and his promises never fail.

He goes on to cleanse and then dress his bride, just as he cleanses us from our pasts and gives us a new wardrobe in Christ: "I bathed you with water and washed the blood from you and put ointments on you. I clothed you with an embroidered dress and put sandals of fine leather on you. I dressed you in fine linen and covered you with costly garments. I adorned you with jewelry: I put bracelets on your arms and a necklace around your neck, and I put a ring on your nose, earrings on your ears and a beautiful crown on your head."

God is pleased to cleanse us from the stains of our pasts and lavish us with new adornments. He loves to dress us in a beautiful gown, new shoes, precious jewels, and a diamond ring. With yet another expression of his love, he even feeds us with fine food of olive oil and honey. He spares no expense on us. We go from being naked and bare and kicking about to being perfumed and adorned and crowned as a princess bride.

You cannot slouch when you wear a crown of jewels.
You can only hold your head high.

"You became very beautiful and rose to be a queen," the Lord says. "And your fame spread among the nations on account of your beauty, because the splendor I had given you made your beauty perfect" (Ezekiel 16:1-14).

The King of Kings Speaks

I wore a crown of piercing thorns so you could wear a crown of priceless jewels.

I wasn't the kind of king they were looking for, you know. I was much smaller. They thought I would come like a supernova shooting through the night sky. They thought I would come as a commanding ruler in majesty and authority.

But I came like a dimly lit candle, a small, flickering light—just as you came, a newborn baby. There was no room for me in the inn.

In my time as a man, I found there was little room in the world for me either. There I was, the Son of Man, in skin. Though some of my brothers recognized me right away and loved me, many more mocked and insulted me. Most despised me. Their hearts were hard.

I came like they did, a humble and helpless child, so they would know I understood their sorrow and their shame, their burdens and their flesh.

They pictured me as enthroned with a king's scepter. But they got a carpenter. They expected a ruler, but got a servant; a holy lord, but got a hilltop preacher; a saint, but got a friend of sinners; a king, but got a champion of the poor. They expected more, but I chose to be less.

But they didn't define me; my Father did.

With each lashing, I felt your rejection and pain. I felt the way you were abandoned and alone, even the way you felt far from God. I felt what it's like to long for man's love and not get it. I know what it feels like to love so deeply, so hard, so raw, and so real and yet be spit upon. I know what it feels like to offer forgiveness but in turn be condemned.

To give grace as man turns his face against you.

To bless and be cursed by those you called friends.

And I know what love is: believing, trusting, suffering long, and never giving up hope.

I promise: I will come back for you like a shooting star blazing through the blue-black sky. You'll know it's me. On my thigh and on my robe I have this name written: King of Kings.

The apostle John writes in Revelation, "His eyes are like blazing fire, and on his head are many crowns...He is dressed in a robe dipped in blood, and his name is the Word of God. The armies of heaven were following him, riding on white horses and dressed in fine linen, white and clean. Coming out of his mouth is a sharp sword...On his robe and on his thigh he has this name written: KING OF KINGS AND LORD OF LORDS" (Revelation 19:12-16).

The men in your life may be incredible, but they don't have eyes like blazing fire. Your best friend may trust God with all his heart, but he doesn't have a double-edged sword coming out of his mouth. Your father may pray every night, but he doesn't wear many crowns. Your boyfriend may love you to the moon and back, but he's not dressed in a robe dipped in blood.

Do you see the difference between men and God? Men can be warriors—fierce, protective, even dying in battle for our freedom. But only God is the King of Kings, the ruler of the universe who never changes or fades or dies.

A Beloved Daughter

In his writing, the apostle John never referred to himself as "John." Instead, he called himself "the beloved of the Lord" or "the one the Lord loved." Did he think the Lord loved him more than the other disciples? Was he just full of himself?

I don't think so. I think he knew how wide, how deep, how great is the river of Christ's love for his children, and he planted himself in it. He wrote, "See what great love the Father has lavished on us, that we should be called children of God! And that is what we are!" (1 John 3:1).

When Jesus died on the cross, he cried out, "Abba, Father!" *Abba* means "Daddy." Some of us need a new picture of Daddy. I give you this picture of Shane with our first child, Olivia, not because they're perfect, but because it's a perfect picture of the Daddy's heart for his daughters.

Shane carries our brand-new baby girl up the narrow walkway to the front door. As I follow behind him, he has her wrapped tightly in her blanket. He is holding her close to his heart like she is the most delicate creature he's ever laid his hands on, which, of course, she is. She is his beloved daughter.

When he reaches the doorstep, he suddenly stops and grips her closer to his chest.

"What am I going to do when some guy comes knocking at the front door for her?" He panics. He is probably picturing himself with a rifle, standing between that future boy and his daughter's heart. He is dead serious about guarding her heart, and he knows full well that means guarding her body. He is her father and that comes as naturally to him as hunting deer.

Of course, my concern at that point is not her dating.

"Babe, she is three days old," I say, ushering him through the doorway. "All she needs right now is a nap!" I shoo him along and put her down in her crib, in the beautiful room we have prepared for her.

We call Olivia our little ladybug. At night she curls up on Daddy's chest and sleeps with her head on his beating heart. He strokes her back and looks down at her and smiles.

When Olivia is just 18 months old, Daddy starts taking her on dates. He calls her from work and asks her on a proper date, and she accepts. When the evening comes, he is dressed very nicely. He approaches her bedroom door right on time.

Olivia never wants him to see her until she is completely ready; she is like a princess in her chamber. I braid her hair and help her put on her favorite outfit. Sometimes it's pink cowboy boots and jeans, sometimes a sundress, sometimes black patent leather shoes and a satin skirt. No matter, she prances out like she is the most prized child in all the world.

On their dates, Daddy opens the door for her. Daddy notices her outfit and compliments her smile. Daddy takes her someplace special and they eat something yummy. Daddy asks her questions and looks her in the eye and listens for her answers. Whether it's pizza and pinball, the fair or a dance, for that moment, there is nothing that matters more than her.

They never skip dessert: ice cream or warm gooey cookies or chocolate soufflé that oozes a heavenly drizzle. Their time together is marked by friendship and laughter and fun: It's a daddy–daughter date.

At the end of the evening, they buy flowers for her and Mommy too.

When Olivia is tucked in and I finish arranging her flowers so she can

*see them from her bed, I lean over to kiss her goodnight. I can see in her face
the security of knowing she is loved.*

*Of course in the back of his mind, Shane is thinking, "If some guy
doesn't pick her up on time or tries to text her for a date or doesn't open the
door for her or tries to get away with not paying for her meal or treating
her like a princess, she'll know who to call! She'll call me, and I'll come rescue her!"*

You don't have to have an earthly daddy to know your heavenly
Daddy's heart for you. When you put your faith in his Son, the Father
comes and makes his home in you by giving you his Spirit. By the Spirit
of Christ, you too can cry, "Abba, Father!" because whether or not you
were "Daddy's little girl" on earth, you are in heaven.

Secure in Love

Are you secure in God's love for you? I spent too many seasons of
my life in insecurity. I put too much of my security in people. The only
constant security we can have is God's love for us.

One of my favorite verses, Deuteronomy 33:12, offers us a picture
of finding our security in our identity as God's beloved daughters:

> Let the beloved of the LORD rest secure in him,
> for he shields [her] all day long,
> and the one the LORD loves rests between his shoulders.

As you read this verse, picture yourself crawling up into the Father's
lap, resting your head between his strong shoulders, and laying the side
of your face on his big beating heart. There you can cry, you can laugh,
and you can be yourself without fear of judgment or rejection.

You have all the attributes of a princess—
hope, dreams, and a future.

You are the beloved of the Lord. His cherished daughter. You can rest secure in that. Root yourself in his love. Establish yourself in it like a tree. If you do, you will flourish.

When a woman is rooted well, she stands tall. You cannot slouch when you wear a crown of jewels. You can only hold your head high as the beloved daughter of the King.

3 The Second Lie:

You Are What You See in the Mirror

That mean ol' mirror is always changing.

Magic Mirror on the Wall

I see every bulge. Every blemish. Every ripple of cellulite, every line, curvy, straight, deep, superficial. Every droop, every sag, every scar, every way this body refuses to cooperate with what I want it to be. I see where this top clings to the wrong places and all the ways I do not match the airbrushed beauty in the magazine. I see how my body compares to hers, and how hers compares to mine. I see how I am different from her in a millisecond.

I know what it's like to look in the mirror and analyze. To worship the self, the body, and to think, even for a moment, that it reflects your value. I know how a mirror can make you feel ugly and gross. I know what it's like to feast my eyes on other girls and compare. By looking at them, I'm not criticizing them; I'm criticizing me. I'm hating what's not right about me. Me, me, me. The mirror makes me fixate on myself— as if the whole world's gaze is fixed on my pimples or frizz, as if the whole world must stop and decide how I look in this outfit.

In the modeling industry, that was my job—to compare myself, to look better. Over time I felt like I could never measure up to the perfection expected of me. I felt like throwing a rock at the mirror and watching it shatter into a million pieces on the ground.

It went like this: one day, pretty; the next, not. If I got so skinny that you could see all my ribs, I'd lose my boobs. If I starved till my stomach was completely flat, I'd have no plump in my face and look tired. If I worked out till I was exhausted, dark circles framed my young eyes.

Why isn't healthy beautiful? When I'm healthy, I'm not a size 4. I'm an 8. When I'm happy, I eat. When I'm really happy, I'm not stressed about working out—it just feels good. When I'm beautiful enough, I'll let you know. When not one day, not two days, not even two weeks, but two years goes by, and I feel beautiful every day, I'll drop you a note, but don't hold your breath.

The mirror is a liar! So is the camera lens. Liars, liars, pants on fire. What if we all decided the mirror is a big fat liar? What if I was more than what I look like, and so are you?

Your body is not a measure of your beauty. Instead, God places your heart on a scale. If you could see my heart you would see it's not really my looks I'm worried about. I'm terrified that promises might not come true and I might get hurt and love might not prevail. My heart is not weighed down by pounds but by anxiety. My heart fears. That's why I don't feel beautiful. That's why.

Happy Now?

Nina wraps the measuring tape around my waist, cinching it closed with the clink of her porcelain nails: 28"

She pencils the numbers on her notepad.

Breasts: 36"

Waist: 28"

Hips: 36"

Sliding the silver weight of the scale, click, click, tap: 141.

Height: 6'

"I'd like to see you lose one and a half inches in your waist, two inches in your hips, and get down to 125," she says matter-of-factly. "That would be ideal."

"How is she going to lose fifteen pounds? Where can she take two inches off her hips?" my father asks, as if someone is going to pipe up and agree with him.

"Working out," she announces. "Swimming is the absolute best way to shed pounds."

None of us challenge the empress of the modeling world. Obviously, I will need to obey her.

"Mark my words"—she shakes her finger at us—"she'll be on the cover of *Vogue* by the end of the summer."

Our eyes get big.

I'd better start running, I think, *or find myself a pool.*

Nina calls me over to the light box to look at my pictures.

"Do you see this extra flesh along here?" she points out, running her long, red fingernail down the photograph, tracing my inner thigh. "You've got to tone this."

"See this?" She points out the lack of definition in my upper arm, the little bulge around my middle, the undefined shape of my calf.

She has me look through the magnifier to see how I wrinkle my nose when I smile.

"You can't do that," she tells me. "No wrinkling."

Check, check, check, check, I thought.

It is Fashion Week, five years later, and I am running through the central park of Milan, Italy. I am 22, have graduated from college, and have come to Milan to hit the runway. Pushing myself to sprint around the trails, I ignore my hunger and avoid eye contact with the happy couples gnawing lazily on their pizza, relaxing on their picnic blankets. Their children toddle about, faces slopped with gelato. I have no time or energy to waste longing for what they have. I have to run.

Thousands of models are in town. Their long, toned legs strut the sidewalks of the fashion district. By day, they crowd the agencies, casting rooms, and hotel foyers, gripping their portfolios, looking in the mirror, checking appointments. In the afternoons, their svelte bodies are draped all over the sidewalk cafes. By night they consort with Italian men over glamorous dinner parties. Some are young and innocent; others are hard and chiseled veterans not begging for anybody's love. We all have this in common: we want a place on that catwalk and would be happy to snatch it from another girl, no matter how hard she worked to get here.

My journey through Fashion Week pinnacles when I meet the king of this play: the famed designer Armani. His sky blue eyes, silver hair, sunbaked skin, and judicious gaze are matched only by the exquisite tailoring of his suit.

He likes my skeleton frame. He chooses to design the makeup and hair for the shows on the palette of me. He uses me to announce his new line to the press. He picks me to be first to step on the stage. When I look in the mirror of his studio, I think I am *more* because of my reflection: I see the jeweled bustier, the painted eyes, the elaborate hair, curls pinned like a crown.

After the shows, I feel a mix of pride and guilt. What I see on the stage is that glamour and glitz elicit applause. Yet what I see backstage haunts me. The sight of the girls' rib cages, spines like knuckles down their backs, bones for thighs...these images imprint themselves in my mind. At any moment, I can recall the image of envy in my roommates' faces when they discovered I landed the shows and they got none. With my heart I see the flowing tears of the girl who lived across the hall. Her long blonde tresses framed a crushed spirit: She had starved herself for Armani only to be eliminated by him. Their eyes, their skin, their souls root themselves in my heart.

Even when the shows are over, I keep up the habit of eccentric self-denial. I deny food like I deny happiness.

I stand on the scale in the gym in Milan. The doctor barred me from the steam room due to my shockingly low blood pressure. Carefully, I tap the silver bar on the scale to the left, to the left, to the left, surpassing Nina's numbers by a longshot.

"There you go, Nina," I whisper. "Happy now?"

I look over my shoulder to make sure no one sees me and sneak into the steam room. Sweating, I sit, spine hunched forward, hands gripping what's left of my thighs. I run my fingers over the hollow curve of my empty belly and up my rib cage. I can feel each bone but still pinch the stubborn flesh clinging around the belly button.

It started out just losing college weight. When I left for Italy, I was fit, tan, and strong. Now I'm emaciated, pale, and weak. All but Armani keep telling me I should eat, I've lost weight in my face, I look sick. Someone even said I'm so skinny a man could never love me like this. But they are wrong. I am booked solid for months.

Yet on the jobs, fabrics begin to drape off me as from a wire hanger; the designers complain. I don't fill out the tops, the pants, the gowns. Makeup artists snicker at my bones, muttering under their breath that I am sick. I am critiqued, analyzed, and discarded by more and more people whose job it is to choose the right girl for the right picture. But as they analyze my body many seem unaware I have a tender heart connected to it. Most are just looking for the right mannequin and it's not their fault if I'm not what they want. And I don't care what they think. I don't care if they tell me to eat. I'm not hungry. I'm not.

But I am. I am hungry for none of this to matter. For the flesh around my middle to be all right. That's where I carry my organs, after all, and women should be allowed to have that. I'm hungry for someone to look into my eyes and tell me I'm beautiful—not because of what they see, but for who I am beneath this skin.

I'm starving to laugh and eat and play and frolic and for no one to care how the clothes fit me. I want to be loved for more than how I look…but how I look seems like the only way to get love.

I dive into the swimming pool. If I swim for an hour or two, if I shed the pounds, if I drown out their voices under water, that's an answer, right?

Soul Hunger

Eating disorders are holes in the soul, not holes in the belly. What we must understand is where the holes come from. The soul has a natural hunger to be affirmed, loved, and protected. When those hungers are not met, we look for something else to fill us. The world dishes out approval for skinny models so we believe a lie: We can fill our soul hunger by controlling our bodies.

Common denominators of girls at war with their bodies are

loneliness, the quest for approval, a desire for control, a focus on the self, and a need to be heard.

I want to be loved for more than how I look.

At my worst hour in my battle against my body, I felt completely alone and isolated, like I was on an island calling for someone to row their boat to me and take me away from the pain, but no one heard my cries. The problem was, I didn't cry loud enough; I muffled my own voice for fear I would have to face the darkness within me.

While loneliness is a likely companion in eating disorders, the need for approval is at their root. When our natural longing to be approved of is not met, it can grow to titanic proportions. My friend Gayle spun into an eating disorder when her older brother told her she would be beautiful if she grew her hair out and lost ten pounds. She did what he said, but there was no destination point—there never is. *At what point am I good enough?* she asked. *At what point am I beautiful?*

Gayle dropped to a staggering 98 pounds. Always longing for her father's love, Gayle received nothing but rejection and disapproval from him. When he abandoned her family to start a new one, Gayle's mother grew morbidly obese, depressed, and disengaged. Rejecting her mother's obesity, Gayle starved herself and then became bulimic to hide her illness, binging and purging on Big Macs and desserts sometimes fifteen times a day. When she did try to get her mother's attention, she was only criticized.

"I was never good enough," Gayle winces. As a grown woman, it still hurts.

I remember this. I remember going to sleep hungry. I remember the darkness, the rebellion, the distance I put between myself and goodness. I remember starving myself to please the mirror and how the mirror turned around and became my enemy. It changed my reflection to the point where I could not see who I was, what I was made of, and the wretch I was becoming.

We long to be affirmed, yet when conditions are placed upon that affirmation, we believe we are worth wherever we land on the measuring stick of the standards set for us.

When our lives spin out of control, we are like girls at amusement parks holding on for dear life. If we can control something—like what goes into our bodies and what comes out of them—we feel like everything is going to be okay.

But we cannot control others, and even though we trick ourselves into thinking we can control our bodies, we cannot. Instead, the issues with food control us and start to suffocate us. As Gayle says, "The rope you're holding on to suddenly becomes a noose."

In the modeling world, I wanted approval like I wanted air. When the approval began to dry up, I continued to do the one thing that earned me applause in the first place: I worked out; I lost weight. I covered my hurt with makeup and tried to make pretty. But pretty is as pretty does, and pretty it wasn't.

Eating disorders never stand alone; there is always a deeper need for love at stake.

I ran home for Christmas to get my footing. When I stepped off the plane, my father was shocked by my dark, hollow eyes and withered stature. While at home, I answered my parents' questions elusively; I did not speak directly of my pain or tell the stories that stirred in my soul. I said nothing about the tormenting images I saw behind the scenes of the modeling world and how my heart felt anguished by them. I avoided eye contact and covered my illness by eating heartily for a brief time.

My family did not address things face to face; back then we skirted around truth like one might sidestep a ditch. We pretended things were okay when they were not okay—not even close to okay.

My parents commented on how skinny I was, but the thing they focused on was my skin. I had battled mild acne as a teen, but in the midst of my illness, cystic acne was emerging on my chin, cheeks, and forehead, my body's hormonal response to lack of nutrition. My hair was growing tawny and dim; my eyes were lightless. Depression reeked from me. My mother made me an appointment with my childhood pediatrician.

I stood before him barefoot on the cold tile floor, the childish wallpaper echoing a simple past. His brow cinches as he examines not only the glaring pimples on my face but the muddy color around my eyes. His old, calloused fingers run along my spine and brush my upper arm. As he examines me, I believe he is looking for that little girl who used to bound into his office with curly blonde pigtails, plump thighs, and big sapphire eyes.

"What can we do about these pimples?" my mother and I ask—they don't work in a model's life.

He scans the sores on my face. "For these, I can prescribe antibiotics. It will take time, but they will eventually clear." He wraps his fingers around my forearm and brushes my lower leg. "It's not her skin I'm worried about. It's her weight. And the foul odor of her breath. Are you ingesting chromium?" he asks me.

"Yes," I answer. Chromium is the main ingredient in my fat burners.

"You are taking far too much. When was the last time you menstruated?"

"I can't remember," I respond. "Maybe six months ago."

His concerned eyes divert to my mother. "Does she have to go back to Europe?" he asks.

Of course we believed that I did. None of us wanted to face the ugly fact that I was beginning to suffer from anorexia, taking fat burners when there was no fat to burn. We all believed the Armani spring shows were too important and I had to go back.

Either we could not see or did not want to see what the doctor saw so clearly. Why does the world tug so hard on us that we refuse to address the most important thing, the truth standing in front of us, barefoot on the tile floor?

The very next season back in Milan, my waist was an inch thicker, my eyes were three shades darker, and I was lonelier to the sixth degree.

Armani could see it. He cancelled me for the shows and removed me from a huge print campaign. The men at the agency were furious. They said I was anorexic, had acne, and didn't look like the girl in my pictures anymore. New models were coming to town. What did they need a girl in pain for? I had lost my beauty. In that world, I had lost my value.

Eating disorders attack like a snake. They sink their venomous fangs into us, draining us. At first we think we look better, but they keep sucking our blood. The poison leaves us lifeless and sick.

An Unkind Friend

We need to know we matter. When we do not know that, the void is a massive black hole we climb into, and we think we cannot get out. When my friend Kaylie was growing up, food brought comfort in an unsafe environment. At home, she lacked the freedom to voice her pain. Feelings and emotions were denied and she felt like she couldn't speak. As a teen, she had a subtle awareness of her weight, but when she went to cosmetology school and found herself faced with the mirror every day, she became exceedingly aware of her body and frame. The girls compared themselves to one another, trying to measure up to what beauty is supposed to look like.

I'm hungry for someone to look into my eyes and
tell me I'm beautiful—not because of what they see,
but for who I am beneath this skin.

Every day as a hair dresser, Kaylie is faced with the mirror. The mirror became a friend to her as she tried to find her identity. It was a safe place to answer her questions, *Who is this girl? Where does she belong? How does she fit in?*

Hair, makeup, and fashion became a way for Kaylie to speak when she didn't know what to say. She began not eating enough, and when life got hard and circumstances threatened to suffocate her, binging and purging became a way to grasp control—until it controlled her.

"It starts before the binging and purging," Kaylie says. "It starts when you turn inward, when food or weight or size or your reflection becomes your source of fulfillment.

"It's selfish. You are dwelling on yourself, your body, and what people think of you. It's all about you. And it steals a moment of your life that God created for you to enjoy and embrace. But instead of experiencing that joy, you look inward, selfishly trying to change something about yourself to receive acceptance from others. Or you try to disappear from a moment that is really a gift from God."

The mirror becomes a friend who reflects your value. But it's an unkind friend, because it's never satisfied, and it's always changing its opinion of you.

We need to know we matter.

The reflection in the mirror will change your entire life. You are always growing older, and you do not look the same from year to year. Do you look the same now as you did when you were a toddler? And when you're 30, will you still look like a teenager? How about when you're 60? How about 80?

I know what it's like to be young and to want perfection, and to realize it's not possible. I know what it's like to compare and compete, to want the mirror to give me what I want and find out it's only glass. Glass gets foggy. Glass cracks. Glass cuts. Glass won't change its reflection of me no matter how hard I wish it would.

But glass doesn't make me or break me anymore, because I can't define myself by what I see. I have to define myself by what I cannot see, and decide to see myself through God's eyes. As *The Little Prince* puts it, "It is only with the heart that one can see rightly; what is essential is invisible to the eye."*

I can't define myself by what I see.

What would happen if we turned away from the slave in the mirror and shifted our gaze to a mirror that always accepts us and never changes its mind about us?

Is there really a mirror like that? A mirror that is satisfied? A mirror that reflects who we are and what we are worth?

Yes, there is.

---

* Antoine de Saint Exupéry, *The Little Prince* (London: Wordsworth Editions Ltd., 1958), 82.

The Second Truth:

You Are a Precious Creation

*We are the clay, you are the potter; we
are all the work of your hand.*

Isaiah 64:8

Barbie in the Kitchen

I look like I should be standing on top of a cake. I am wearing a pastel pink gown, hoopskirt, and raspberry petticoats. My hair is piled high in a puffy up-do. It is the thirty-fifth anniversary of the Barbie doll, and I am it, her, the doll beneath the dress.

They needed a hungry girl to play Barbie. They found one.

The hair stylist and makeup artist work for three hours, covering the dark circles under my eyes, masking the acne on my cheeks, smoothing my kinky hair into a perfect bouffant. As I look in the mirror, I do not love what I see; I see an empty shell. On the inside, I cry. I don't know where the tears come from; I have yet to delve into the secret layers of my heart.

When they present me as Barbie, children run toward me. They all want to touch the silk of my gown. They want me to look them in the eyes and smile. When I do, I know they are duped; but right now, I can see clearly. Beautiful isn't Barbie; beautiful is the gleam of hope I see in the children's eyes.

Being Barbie is the seed from which my later passion grows. It is the seed of knowing what it's like to hurt on the inside while we mask the outside.

Beautiful isn't Barbie. Beautiful is the gleam of hope
I see in the children's eyes.

Years later, after I leave the modeling industry, my heart grows tender each time I hear the story of a girl who doesn't feel like she's enough. I care that some girls ache to be Barbie. I want to tell them Barbie isn't beautiful; they are. I want to tell every girl on earth.

❧

When I first began reading the Bible, it felt like someone was feeding the empty belly of my ravished spirit with morsels of bread dipped in sweet oil. I savored the tang of grace and hungered for more. I began to turn away from the mirror of the world to the mirror of God. My attention diverted from how I looked to how he looked and how he viewed me.

Leaving the modeling industry was no simple step. I had been building my career for 15 years, and turning away with no one's permission was one of the most courageous things I've ever done. At the same time, it was simple: I was leaving in pursuit of God's dreams for me, and his dreams seemed like a greater adventure with a greater destination.

Before I came home, my mother vacationed to Italy to see me and we went to the South. There we met a wrinkly Italian grandmother who reacquainted me with the meaning of *home*. Little dogs scurried around her tiny house and a mouth-watering aroma drifted from her kitchen. The runways of Milan were worlds away. The grandmother grew sweet, juicy oranges and ruby red tomatoes in her backyard. Her chubby hands ground her own flour and pressed the dough of her homemade pasta. She pureed rich tomato sauce from scratch, served hand-pressed golden olive oil straight from the farmer, and baked her own crusty bread. As I watched her stir the red sauce with a worn wooden spoon, I knew I had to return home, to my own mother and grandmother, to God, to family, and to the kitchen.

When my feet landed back in the United States for good, I came home to what I had known as a child—my mother cooking in the kitchen, making three square meals a day. On Sundays, Mom baked flats of seasoned bone-in chicken until the whole kitchen filled with the scent of crisp brown skin and juices steaming in the pan. She made thick, cheesy, sausage-stuffed lasagna. Pea soup with ham hock and thyme. Gooey fudge brownies, carrot cake with cream cheese frosting, pumpkin bread, zucchini bread, banana bread galore. As a little girl I used to help her mix in the nuts, lick the bowl and spoon, and peek over the countertop at the steaming cakes.

These days I spend a lot of time in my husband's mother's kitchen. On any given holiday she will decorate the table like sweet Jesus is coming for dinner. Her Thanksgivings are filled with a brown-sugar crusted sweet potato casserole, a tender brined turkey, rich giblet gravy, perfectly whipped potatoes, and rolls steaming from the oven. There is nothing so sweet as Linda's famous chocolate pie, made from a recipe handed down from Grandma Inez—a recipe I am teaching my daughter.

As we stand in Linda's kitchen, our words mingle like cups of flour, tablespoons of sugar, and pinches of salt, combining to make a new recipe. When times are confusing, we just stir the sauce and check the meat and make small talk. Sometimes we even foresee answered prayers when nothing points to them. Even in the most difficult times, we will cook a perfect roast, knowing blessings await on the other side of heaven.

When I was modeling, beating my body with starvation and over-exercise became a way for me to put a big red punching bag on my fist and pound at whatever I wanted. But I was only bruising myself.

When we turn against ourselves, we are angry that we do not have the love we need. When we choose to be sick, we reap the fruit of that choice—and the fruit is rotten. When we choose life and wellness, we reap the fruit of that choice as well, and the fruit is sweet and satisfying.

I chose Christ. I picked life.

When I left the modeling industry, I left anorexia. I left the fruitless lie that my body wasn't good enough. I walked away from a life based on appearance. I ditched the poisonous idea that my value rested in the bathroom mirror. I chose Christ; I picked life.

When we have the opportunity to choose, we must choose life. We must choose the abundant road that will lead to the deep, rich fruit we desire. It will also, by the way, include lots of time in the kitchen—dicing vegetables, stirring sauces, seasoning dishes, setting, serving, cleaning, and laughing around the table.

When life isn't what you wish it would be, sometimes you need to just buck up and make a decision. In the case of battles we wage on our own bodies, we can either pick sickness or pick health. You can either pursue illness, feeding its unquenchable fire, or pursue happiness. Sometimes it's good to forecast the end result of the choice you make. Picture life at the end of the sickness road, the one that focuses on self. Imagine the destination of that road in depth. Then, picture life at the end of the wellness road, the one that focuses on blessing others. Sketch it; dream it; write it. Which end do you want? It's your choice.

If you have to push through the crowd and beg God to split the Red Sea to reach healing, do it. Do whatever you have to do to get well. Freedom awaits on the other side of the reach.

A Fast from the Mirror

Ten years after I leave the modeling industry, I am writing my story. The more I write, the more the hurt surfaces. The more the hurt surfaces, the more my skin breaks out. The more my skin breaks out, the more creams I try. I try peels, medicine, and treatments, but the acne only multiplies.

I stare at the mirror and can hardly stand what I see. My skin, once creamy and soft, is riddled with sores. Pimples mar my forehead, cheekbones, and jawline, rearing their blaring faces on either side of my mouth. They are cystic and vile, clustering in pocks. I hate these ugly sores. I hate looking at myself—and the more I do, the bigger they get, and the greater the intensity of the anxiety creeping down my neck.

Mortified, I barely leave the house. When my husband comes home, I shrink back in shame and cover my face. The treatments have made my skin so dry that I can peel it off like snakeskin. My kids want to know "what is wrong with Mommy's face."

Under a starry black sky, I pound my fists on the backyard deck, begging God to heal me.

In a final plea for help, I drive hours to meet a famous dermatologist. Surely he will fix me; he will give me a magic prescription to make this torture go away.

He examines me closely. He notices not only my sores but my distress. As I describe my experience, tears rush to my eyes. I can barely speak.

"My dear," he says compassionately, "you are not an acne patient. You are a heart patient."

I lean closer to make sure he sees the pimples ruining my face.

"Your issue originates not in the skin. It is in the heart and mind," he says.

I start talking and don't even know what comes out. I slobber all over my words and have to collect myself with tissue. The doctor prescribes a hormone therapy which will take until Easter to work. It's not even Thanksgiving yet.

I am panicked. My face is marred. I want a prescription to heal this *now*. Instead, he recommends counseling. "Once the emotional healing comes," he says, "the physical healing will follow."

He sends me across the hall to an esthetician. As I am lying on the table I'm hoping she will recommend a magic cream that will put a stop to this nonsense. She doesn't. Instead she tells me to stop look-ing in the mirror.

"Take a month off," she says with quiet music playing in the back-ground. "Do what you love; focus on what makes you happy. Don't look."

I cry half the way home and start my fast from the mirror by the time I pull into the driveway.

When I get home, I announce that we will no longer focus on my skin. "I am more than my skin," I tell my children.

For forty days, I don't look. In the morning, I pop in my contacts in dim lighting, barely tame my hair, and forgo makeup; my face is too much of a mess for makeup anyway. In place of that time, I do what I love: I read the Word and write. I learn to turn away. Realizing I glance at my reflection in the rearview mirror to "check" my skin, I tilt the mirror away so I can't see. I stop glancing at my reflection in car win-dows and shops.

About three weeks into the fast I am dropping my son off at pre-school and see his teacher.

"Jen!" she exclaims. "You look radiant! What have you been doing?"

That morning, I had been reading the Word. The Bible says it gives light to the eyes and radiance to the face. Moses was so radiant after going face to face with God that he had to wear a veil.

Do you really think beauty is a woman who looks like
a doll instead of a child with a chocolate-smeared
smile looking up at the moon?

Something happened on my fast. I found out what I love and what makes me happy. I didn't find that from looking in the mirror or focus-ing on myself. I found it from turning away from the mirror and look-ing into the One who never changes. Aside from reading the Word night and day, I tromped the mountain trails and counted stars over the lake. I laughed with my kids and forgot what I looked like. I wrote my heart out. I finally told my story.

When the emotional healing came, the physical healing followed. I learned a lot about beauty during that fast. It changed the way I saw beauty and changed the way I saw myself.

That must be a little of what the blind experience; they learn to see with their hearts.

The Creator Speaks

My daughter, I see how you worry about things you cannot control. Surrender control. Give me the reins. Let go of your body and all its regulations. I made it; I formed it; I know it best.

Do you really think beauty is a woman who looks like a doll instead of a child with a chocolate-smeared smile looking up at the moon?

Do you really think your imperfections point to my inability? That because I didn't make you perfect, I am not a good artist?

I know what beauty is. I allow trees to shed their leaves so children can dance a crunchy jig in them. I give a girl the voice of an angel, a body to twirl across the stage, a lemon chiffon sunrise to remind her of me. Night and day I splatter the world with my name: Creator.

I wove you together in the depths of the earth; I crafted you. You are my poetry, my creation. You are a handcrafted vase, a tapestry with a dream stitched through your heart. You are blonde, brunette, wide-eyed. You are tall, voluptuous, small-framed, and smart. You are the next generation of writers, dreamers, dancers, singers, teachers, and world changers. My people make up the kaleidoscope of who I am—together, you are the image of me.

Yet sorrow flows in a crimson tide when I see my children squandering their wonderful bodies like they are trash. When you abuse yourself, it hurts me, and I want you to know it.

I hear the world saying, "It's your body; you can do whatever you want with it!" But I don't say that. Did you make your body? Did you fashion it with your hands? Did you buy it from me? What price did you pay?

I paid the price. I spent everything I had on you. I received the whipping on my own flesh to buy back yours. I am your Maker and your body is my creation. When I craft a masterpiece, I am proud of my design. I did a fine job on you, and I still am working.

Reaching for the Healer

There is a story in the Bible about a woman who had been bleeding for twelve years. When Jesus came to her town, she pressed through the crowd to get to him, thinking if she just touched the edge of his robe she would be healed. When she touched his garment, the suffering in her body ceased. Years of belittlement and rejection, years of emotional bleeding, and years of being out of control in her body came to an end.

Instead of grasping for control over a body she could not control, she reached for him—the One who made her body and the only one who could heal it. But Jesus wasn't content to go on his merry way, forgetting all about her. He wanted to see her face. He stopped for her. He searched for her in the crowd. When he found her, she came to him trembling, and told the whole truth.

In return, he called her "Daughter." In the mirror of his face she saw who she truly was. She was not just a messy, imperfect girl who would never be cherished. She was precious to him, his creation, fashioned with his very hands. She was more than her body; she had a soul. She had courage to push through the crowd, not caring what anyone else thought anymore, and press in to Jesus. What did she get in return? A new diet? A new medicine? A new workout plan? No. He blessed her with freedom and peace.

I remember reaching for the Healer. The moment I cried out, he heard me. Over time, I told my "whole truth" and he gave me that freedom and peace to know he made me just the way he wanted to. I didn't have to be like anyone else anymore. I could just be his daughter, his creation, beautiful to him in my own unique way.

My people make up the kaleidoscope of who I am.
Together, you are the image of me.

To find freedom in your body is to accept that it will always be changing and you will never have full control. It is to decide that the mirror, the scale, and the jean size do not define you, but God does. It is to celebrate the Creation you are, realizing you are a splash of color in the artwork of his grand Creation, and you reflect the image of the One who made you.

To find peace in your body is to decide to care for it because you are worth it. To eat healthily, exercise regularly, and enjoy your body because it is your unique expression. My challenge to you is to be the best you can be in the skin you are in. If your mother, grandmother, sisters, and friends and I did that, we could bless the world with more than a dress size or a number on a scale. We could touch the world with our fingerprints, blessing it with beauty that begins with our inward gifts, shining inside and out.

My friend Kaylie still stands in front of the mirror all day as a hairdresser. Because she has reached for the Healer, every person who enters her space enters the presence of their Creator. In her studio, women do not just get their hair done. As many of them battle with their own reflection, she loves and listens and counsels them. They are touched by a woman whose heart, body, and soul have been touched by God.

There is power in reaching for the Healer. When we do, his power reaches back for us, and then reaches out to others through us.

Heaven's Exchange

When I was a little girl, I used to go to my Grandma Betty's house. We would pick strawberries in her strawberry patch and dip them in powdered sugar.

Like a tall candle long burned, my grandmother's whole body

dripped toward the floor. She suffered from osteoporosis and her spine was literally bent over in a hump.

But every time I would visit her, she would look through the peep-hole, swing open the door, and clap her hands in delight. She was all lit up from the inside; her eyes sparkled like sapphires.

Grandma didn't grow up in a world where Botox or spray tans were an option. She practiced standing up straight, ate salmon and spin-ach, did water aerobics, and did her best to keep track of her keys and glasses. She just never got old on the inside. All hunched over but still bright and beautiful, she used to say to me, "You know, I am the same on the inside. I just look different."

The last time I held Grandma, I was nine months pregnant with my daughter, Olivia. Grandma was tired, so I lay on the bed with her and rubbed the tensed muscles around her spine until she drifted off to sleep. Two days later, I gave birth to Olivia just as Grandma was admit-ted to the hospital. She never got out.

When I received the news of Grandma's death, I fell to the ground weeping. All I wanted was for her to get to hold my baby girl, but she never got to.

Yet during those holy hours of caring for Olivia in the middle of the night, touching her soft, tender skin, I felt the mystery of heaven's exchange. At one time Grandma held me; then, as she grew older, I held her. Then, in a way, we both held Olivia, and one day Olivia will hold me. God always exchanges beauty for ashes, and it has nothing to do with what we see in the mirror.

God always exchanges beauty for ashes.

Someday I will see Grandma Betty again, and she'll be standing young and tall. She'll probably look up from her strawberry patch in heaven and clap her hands in sheer delight when she sees me coming.

We are to live by faith, not by sight; to fix our eyes not on what we see, but on what we can't see. What is seen is only temporary, but what is unseen is eternal (2 Corinthians 4:18).

It is a lie to believe beauty is defined only by what is visible. As God crafted the sea and everything in it, he filled us with depths of beauty that cannot be seen on the surface. It's our job to dive into the waters of our souls and discover the treasures there. It's up to us to carry them to the surface and bless the world with their value.

What are you good at? What makes you happy? What love can you share? You are so much more than the sum of your parts.

Embrace the gorgeous truth: You are the Precious Creation of God. The weight of your worth is the weight of your heart; the palm of God, your only scale.

5   The Third Lie:

You Are What Magazines Tell You

The devil is a pretty good liar.

666 Ways to Change You

I have a classic stack of magazines heaped on a shelf in my closet, right next to the pile of my portfolios. The magazines: *Cosmo, Glamour, Vogue, Allure, Seventeen.* The portfolios: Ford, Model Team, Fashion, Nova, Vivian's. Both stacks have something in common; they contain some beautiful lies.

As a teen, I plastered pages torn out from magazines on the back of my bedroom door. Drawn to their perfection, I held these women's faces and bodies as the standard of beauty. When I was modeling as a teen, it was exciting to see myself in the pages of a magazine. Sometimes I liked the pictures; sometimes I didn't. But it was the idea of being in them that was glamorous.

Perfect pictures don't mean girls are perfect.

Over the years of modeling around the world, I became glaringly aware that image does not always match reality. Perfect pictures don't mean girls are perfect. Living with models weighed down by eating disorders, drug abuse, low self-esteem, and a huge need for protection and approval, I had a front row seat to the difference between the regular girls in the models' apartment and the glam girls in the magazines. I grew to understand that magazines make women look flawless when in reality they are just as human as the girls perusing their pages.

The world needs more women looking outward.

It was against this backdrop that I began to look at magazines and be able to rightly understand them.

Here's a sampling of magazine cover titles I have collected over the years:

- 875 Ways to Look Beautiful
- 859 Ways to Look Pretty
- 656 Fashion and Beauty Ideas: Look Pretty Now!
- 624 Ways to Get the Most out of Your Look
- 300 Summer Dresses, Bags, Sandals, Sexy Heels
- 259 New Looks for Every Body and Budget
- 245 Winning Products For the Most Amazing Skin, Hair & Body
- 240+ Shoes, Bags, and New Looks
- How to Get Fresh, Clear Skin; Glossy, Sexy Hair; Fast, Flattering Makeup; A Sleek, Smooth Body; and Bright, Flawless Nails
- How to Dress Thinner and Find the Perfect Jeans
- Your Best Body Ever! Raise Your Metabolism, Get Better Curves, Age-Proof Your Skin!
- The Secret to the Best Behind Ever! Perfect Hair and Gorgeous Glow! Beauty for Under $10!

- Get Everything You Want This Year: Great Body, Tons of $$$, Amazing Clothes, and Mega Confidence!
- What Can You Really Change in 30 Days? A LOT! Fix Your Sex Life, Your Friendships, Your Booty!

As far as I can tell, we have thousands of things we have to do, buy, and change to be satisfied, and the magazines have all the answers.

To be fair, I'm interested in style, design, makeup, hair, and skin. I want great skin, cute outfits, fun shoes, flattering makeup, shiny hair, and a firm behind! But the world is not all about us and how we look; the world needs more women looking outward.

What happens when girls focus inward, on page after page of air-brushed models—along with purses, shoes, jewelry, hair, skin, and clothes which few of us have in real life?

Studies show that after only a few minutes of viewing a fashion magazine, seven out of ten of us begin feeling guilty, depressed, ashamed, and angry. Why? Because we are looking at unrealistic images of beauty that do not match the reflection in the mirror. What the world says is perfect is not what we see in real life.

I believe it is great for us to have a stylish wardrobe, pretty hair and makeup, and take very good care of our bodies. All of that is honorable to our Creator, who adores beauty and loves to adorn us. But should our appearance and adornments be our primary focus? And when women believe what the magazines tell them, are they better for it? Or worse?

Women and girls who read fitness magazines are twice as likely to use unhealthy dieting mechanisms. The countless "health tips" in fitness magazines are outweighed by the feelings readers have when they compare themselves to the images. Women feel they are not enough the way they are and torture themselves to look like the celebrities on the pages.

The question is if we really want to emulate models and celebrities, or if we want to find a unique beauty all our own. The average model does not represent the average woman in America—models are thinner than 98 percent of American women. At least a quarter of the women in Miss

America pageants and *Playboy* centerfolds meet the criteria for anorexia. Is that really attractive? In the world's eyes, yes. In God's eyes, no. There is nothing beautiful about anorexia or bulimia. In a world where children are legitimately starving, eating disorders are twisted and dark.

What is the impact of magazine images on young women? Girls as young as six are dieting. Over half of teens want to lose weight. Girls who are a healthy weight think they are fat. Little girls as young as ten are terrified of being fat, and one in three high school girls shows symptoms of an eating disorder.

I used to be on the covers of magazines, and if I focus for five minutes on the cover girls I start to feel the weight of my flaws. In a snap, I could spiral into comparisons, jealousy, anger, and self-hatred if I looked too long at their flawless skin, hair, and bodies. But I won't, because I know the images aren't true to life. Being in magazines never satisfied me back then, and how I compare to airbrushed images doesn't define me now.

The only one who can sort out
our tangled hearts is God.

Do you ever stop to think about the real lives of women within the pages of magazines? Many of today's cover models have undergone treatment for cutting, emotional instability, drug and alcohol addiction, eating disorders, and physical abuse. Many are in and out of treatment centers, courtrooms, and relationships. Many are so seductive in the public eye, we might understand why their relationships are so complicated and often end in heartbreak.

One *Seventeen* cover girl who is well known for her potty mouth, hard partying, nearly naked fashion statements, and infamous dating violence has titles like these written over her body: "Flirting Moves Guys Find Irresistible." Another star fresh out of rehab poses with *Seventeen* titles like these: "How to Make Guys Worship You" and "Look HOT in a Bikini." What difference does it make if you look hot in a bikini if you are abusing yourself? Why do you want guys to worship you when God's design is for you to have one husband?

The most bizarre issue of all is that in magazines, women don't age. A close examination of a mound of magazine advertisements of celebrities ranging from sixteen to fifty-six years old reveals the power of the airbrush. Whether the woman is in her fifties, forties, or teens, her skin has the exact same texture on the magazine's page. Not one of them has a scar, a crease, a line, a blemish, a wrinkle, or even a strand of hair out of place.

Behind the scenes, celebrities have personal trainers, dieticians, and plastic surgeons and spend large amounts of money on beauty treatments. All of their appearances have been altered by expert makeup artists, hair and clothing stylists, lighting specialists, and photographers. Hundreds of their photos are ditched on the editing room floor, and a single photo is airbrushed to the point of perfection.

I have three all-time favorite cover titles. The first is "Ageless Beauty" on a plastic surgery magazine. (My grandmother never had plastic surgery and her beauty was totally timeless.) The second one is "Instant Happy!" written over a woman airbrushed to look like Barbie. (I *was* Barbie, and I don't buy the lie that happiness is instant.) In yet another, I'm given "176 Tips to Simplify My Life!" written over the image of an unmarried-with-no-children 24-year-old. (Believe me, with a husband, three children, and a career, my life does not have room for 176 tips. My life is already filled with hundreds of things, and only a handful of them give it meaning.)

What's really crazy is this: We haven't even opened the magazines yet.

Cosmo Speaks

Cosmopolitan is the bestselling monthly magazine in the United States. Over 100 million teens and young women in more than 100 nations read *Cosmo*. If we were to gather its readership into one locale, it would be the twelfth-largest country in the world.*

---

* Edith Zimmerman, "99 Ways to Be Naughty in Kazakhstan: How Cosmo Conquered the World," *New York Times,* August 3, 2012.

On a sample of covers, we find starlets who began on *Barney and Friends*, became Disney pop stars, and are now posing to advertise sex. Barely dressed young women are choosing to objectify themselves, and the pop stars, models, and actresses are leading the way. Some of the most favored actresses in Hollywood pose half-dressed on the cover of *Cosmo* with titles like "78 Ways to Turn Him On," "21 Naughty Sex Tips" and "Dirty Lying Brides" written on their bodies. While cover girls don't choose the titles, they know the message of *Cosmo*. Do these teen idols recognize the messages they are sending to 100 million high school and college girls who read these magazines?

What are the messages of *Cosmo?* Let's unpack them. The first message is: Your body is a toy and sex is a game. There is no concept in fashion magazines that your body is a creation of God and sex is a sacred union between husband and wife. The message is that sex is a natural activity that happens often outside of marriage – kind of like going to the gym or getting a massage. What a lie!

Cosmo lies by telling you that your body is your possession. You have the right to do whatever you want with it. Yet, in truth, you didn't make your body and you didn't purchase it, so you don't own it. The Bible teaches your body belongs to God who made it.

The next message of the magazines is: "Your flesh is your value, but your flesh has no value." In other words, your body is your source of worth, but really, it has no worth. You can give it away to guy after guy with no side effects. If this results in an inconvenient pregnancy, according to the magazines, abortion is also an option—therefore your own flesh and blood have no value.

God is not like this. He says, *Your body has value. Your body is my temple. It is holy to me. Sex is holy. Pregnancy is holy. Children are holy.*

Women, not men, produce these magazines. And women, not men, are choosing to objectify themselves in the name of "freedom." But the sexual "freedom" of this generation is actually enslavement.

When young women give their bodies away sexually, they give their hearts and souls too—and often the relationships don't work out, no matter how much they believed it was going to lead to a wedding day.

What are they left with? Heartbreak. Shame. Anger. Betrayal. Disease. An abortion. A shattered dream. And if they end up getting married to the right man later on, they potentially carry all of that garbage into the marriage. Sex outside of marriage can lead to such lifelong pain and regret that all the pages in all the magazines in all the world could not put words to the despair.

Living the *Cosmo* message doesn't work out well for real women. They end up turning their bodies into things, and their hearts get torn in the wake of regret. Then, when they want to clean up their act and find a good husband, they are going to have to search high and low for someone who wants to marry a girl who handed out her body like it was a snack. When the young women who live promiscuously leave college and want to enter into a lifelong committed relationship, that "sexual freedom" does not work well for them. Many struggle deeply to find the true meaning of their lives.

I gave my life to Christ shortly after college and then waited to have sex until after marriage. Aside from leaving the modeling industry, those were the two best decisions I ever made.

Here's my question: when young readers of *Cosmo* go into a marriage carrying the weight of abortions, sexually transmitted diseases, torn relationships, embarrassment, betrayal, and hearts churning with shame, then what? Is *Cosmo* going to help them heal?

I think not. The only one who can heal us is Christ. The only one who can sort out our tangled hearts is God. And the only ones who can pursue his beautiful truth and reject the lies are you and me.

Protect Yourself

In many circles, "protecting yourself" and having "safe sex" means using a condom. But a condom can't protect your heart and does nothing for your future husband's heart. So instead, I advise you to protect yourself by controlling yourself. I advise you to protect yourself by putting firm boundaries around your heart, body, and soul. Do not allow yourself to be alone outside of the public eye with a boy or man, no matter how much you trust him. Do not allow yourself to drink alcohol when out on a date. Choose to not drink at all. Choose to not even touch drugs, which impair your ability to make good choices. I know women who made these choices for themselves and stayed pure till their wedding days. You have the choice to not even put yourself in those positions. If you follow this advice by truly "protecting yourself," believe me, you and your husband will be thankful later when you walk down the aisle. What a beautiful thing for your future husband to know: You are such a courageous woman that you stood up for yourself, you stood out from the crowd, and you preserved the most sacred part of yourself for him.

What if you believed you were worth waiting for?

What if you were different? What if you were a girl who believed she was so valuable she was worth waiting for? If you do, you won't end up with a disease or be faced with the question whether you want to have a baby in high school or college, and you won't face a counselor who gives you the option of abortion.

People who promote sexual "freedom" often consider abortion as the removal of unwanted tissue, kind of like a tonsillectomy. But in truth, abortion is killing a human being. It causes the pregnant woman a tremendous amount of emotional pain that is not removed once the baby is gone.

The other lie promoted by our culture is gender-free sexual partners, as if it doesn't matter if they are male or female. This is called "political correctness." *Glamour* and *Cosmo* promote the idea that it is okay to be bisexual and not limit yourself to one partner at a time.

God created men and women to fit together. You become *one flesh* with the person you have sex with. That's more than a partner. That's a mate who becomes a part of who you are. Why, for example, is it hard for a girl to concentrate on her schoolwork after she's had sex with someone and the relationship ended?

I'll let a young woman answer that question for you. Here is a quote from an eighteen-year-old girl who went to a counseling center for depression and bulimia. Vomiting up to six times a day, the girl said the end of a romance was the source of her pain. During her meeting with the counselor, the girl described her first experience with intimacy:

> When it ended, it hurt so much," she said, weeping. "I think about him all the time, and I haven't been going to one of my classes, because he'll be there, and I can't handle seeing him. I was so unprepared for this...Why, Doctor," she asked, "why do they tell you how to protect your body—from herpes and pregnancy—but they don't tell you what it does to your heart?"

Students are inundated with information about contraception, a healthy diet, the dangers of smoking, the importance of sleep, ways to cope with stress...but not a word about the nightmare that casual sex has on people's emotions.

Why are so many girls broken? Because they believe the lie that it's okay to give their bodies away. And when you give your body away, you give your heart away. You give your soul away. Try telling a girl whose heart was ripped by abortion or date rape or abandonment that sex is safe. Try telling a girl with HPV that sex is safe. Try telling me. You won't get it past me. The world will tell you that safe sex has to do with birth control. But that's a lie. Safe sex has to do with self-control. Safe, protected sex is what happens in a healthy, loving marriage.

A Common Place or a Holy Space?

When I think of a convenience store, I think of a place where everything is common. Nothing is of great value. Everything is cheap and most of it is not good for you. Many young women treat their bodies like they are convenience stores. Boys and men can come in and take what they want and leave them dirty and littered, the floor of their souls matted with sticky footprints and grime. But our bodies are not convenience stores; they are temples. They have value. In fact, they should have guards standing out front because within us lies great treasure and worth, purpose and potential.

Which will you choose? To live like a convenience store, where everything is cheap, easy, and fast? Or to live like a holy place, where everything is so priceless not just anyone can enter in without making a promise to God to treat it like sacred ground?

Let's not let *Cosmo* or the culture tell us what "safe sex" is. Let's let our Creator define that for us. Safe sex happens within safe boundaries—marriage—where the union of God and the church is fully explored and enjoyed. Healthy sex within marriage is a poem, a salve, a bond, and a blast. It is beautiful, it it holy, and it is *so* worth waiting for!

The best way to protect yourself is to protect your marriage, long before you have it. One way is by knowing your enemy—who hates God and hates you and hates the institution of marriage.

The devil is a pretty good liar. The cover girls look glamorous; their seductive outfits and sexual education are syrupy sweet. But beneath the surface we have the same issue we had in the Garden of Eden—the enemy whispering into Eve's ear, convincing her to follow her appetite and make choices separate from her husband and against God's clear boundaries. Because she entertained that pretty little liar, blame, shame, and ugly regret were her adornments.

The original lie is if something looks good, it is good. But the truth is: Just because something looks good or sounds good doesn't mean it *is* good. It may be pretty on the surface, but beneath it you'll find pain you don't want to carry.

Battle Cry

I know I'm pushing this issue hard on you. I know it. But I'm doing it because you matter. Sex matters. Your future husband matters. Your emotional health matters. Your body matters, and your future children matter. That's the truth, and that's why this is my battle cry: Wait for sex because you are worth the wait.

And if you've made mistakes, if you've treated your body more like a common place than a holy place, there is forgiveness for you. Christ broke down the temple so that he could rebuild it. He can do the same with you. If you confess your sin, ask forgiveness, and lay yourself down, he will rebuild you into a temple that honors his name. He died to free you of the consequence of your sin, and he can heal you of its effects.

What if the young women of this generation stood up and said, "I am *more* than my body! I have a heart and mind and spirit! My body is precious and worth saving!" What if we all stood together and cried, "Not me! Not you! Not her! No more! Women are not just things. Women are not just flesh. We are made for more! Our girls are worth venturing into the heart of darkness and rescuing! *Cosmo* lies!"

Together, our voices could speak the real meaning of freedom. Together, we could raise a true battle cry.

It's time for young women to use their voices
to speak truth.

But this isn't just a battle cry for women and girls. It's for men too. Our future husbands and sons deserve it. What the fashion magazines are promoting is not just that women are worthless, but their future husbands are too. Whoever that man is, he deserves to be held in the highest regard. Respecting your husband even before you meet him means believing that not only are you worth the wait, but he is too. He is worth you preserving your body and caring for it like it is a temple, not a convenience store.

A good man is a treasure. Wherever you are in your journey, you would do well to begin treasuring him now.

A Better Headline

It's time for young women to stand up and use their voices to speak truth. It's time for a better headline.

The links between sexual impurity and drug and alcohol abuse, eating disorders, broken hearts, and broken dreams aren't spelled out in the pages of *Seventeen*, *Glamour*, and *Cosmo*, but I've seen the influence of the beautiful lies written on the faces of women and girls. I've looked into their eyes and seen the damage to their hearts. I've read their long, pained letters and held their quivering hands. I've listened to the stories of young women whose eyes are a well of regret and wrapped my arms around the delicate shoulders of weeping girls. I've held grown women in my arms as they sobbed, still shattered by the lie that their body was a toy to be used to please men.

If only the magazines told *their* stories and spelled out *their* voices.

"I Don't Feel Beautiful Enough" could be the lead article. We could tell young women what true beauty is. "Why Does My Heart Hurt Even When My Makeup Looks Perfect?" could be a feature story. "Why Did He Abandon Me After I Gave Him Everything?" could be an article where women's true stories are told.

I can see the titles of the articles I would publish: "Warning! Casual Sex Shouldn't Be Taken Casually!" "12 Ways Sex Outside of Marriage Can Hurt You." "Three Simple Things You Can Do to Stay Pure." "Newsflash: Your Husband Is Worth Waiting for and So Are You!" "You Are Loved! Precious! Sacred, Just as You Are!" "Sex Is Holy! Holy! Holy!" "Your Body Is a Beautiful Temple! Receive Your God-Given Identity *Right Now!*"

6 The Third Truth:

You Are a Beautiful Temple

The glory of the LORD filled the temple.

2 CHRONICLES 7:1

Awesome

I am super tired when I succumb to the desire to lay my head on the couch. I'm supposed to work on the message for my next retreat, but instead I lie down, and instantly a cool wave of relief washes the shore of my mind. I sink into a dream.

I am whisked into a giant meadow. It is so vast, so grand, and so alive, my heart swells with joy. Walking toward me is Jesus. Larger than life, he easily lifts me to his strong shoulders and carries me through the meadow. He carries me high so I can see the endless view. There are mountains and woods in the distance. It is bliss.

I feel the profound satisfaction of heaven. The fullness of joy, the way every need within me is fulfilled.

He calls me by name. "Jen," he says, "Do you want to go to the temple?"

"Yes, Lord! Yes," I say. I love to be in God's house. I adore the temple, and in heaven it would be the first place I would want to go.

So Jesus brings me there, carrying me on his shoulders.

But when we arrive, he is suddenly no longer a man; he is even larger, even greater, a kind of pulsing presence at the center. He is the Lamb, the lamp of heaven.

I am surrounded by a throng of people, masses facing him, their hands raised in worship.

God will go to the end of the earth, to the heart of the blackest night, to rescue his little girls.

It's crazy, I know, but I can't leave this part out. From the center, he looks at me and winks, as if to say, "Isn't it awesome?"

It is awesome! I raise my hands, singing "Holy!"

We, the people, are the precious stones that make up the temple floor. And he is all we need.

The temple is a holy shrine. A sacred space. Priceless in every way.

Polly's Secret

As a young woman, my friend Polly was treated like she was a convenience store and not a temple. She began to believe the lie that her body was her source of worth, yet worthless at the same time. But her story shows the power of the Lamb who takes all ugliness, nails it to the cross, and brings beauty.

At the mere age of seven, Polly was victimized by a grown man. For fear that he would hurt her again, she told no one about the abuse and kept her secret buried so deep that it didn't surface until she was a young woman. At eleven she began using drugs and alcohol, and by eighteen she was a full-blown alcoholic, dancing in the nude as men jeered her on.

A counselor helped Polly see that the sexual part of her was awakened far too soon, which resulted in her destructive lifestyle. As the Bible says, "Do not arouse or awaken love until it so desires" (Song of Songs 8:4). Why are we charged with this? Because when sexuality is aroused before the time of sanctified sex under the covenant of marriage, destruction is the result.

On the stage, Polly danced seductively while men hurled sick and twisted insults at her. She believed the lie that her body was a toy to be used to please men, and it ruined her. "Backstage it is so ugly," she says, "and the girls are broken. I was giving my heart and soul to these men, thinking I was in control, but I wasn't. I sold my soul." She wipes away the tears streaming down her face.

"I felt worthless, like I had no value, and all I wanted was love." She became so empty that one day she drove around in her car with a gun on her lap, planning to end her suffering.

But instead she gave the gun back and started her life again. Her life changed when she discovered she was pregnant with twin girls and married their father. For years she continued to drink, resulting in a depression so dark it nearly crushed her. Her husband wanted her to go church, and they began their journey to the heart of Christ. But then Polly was diagnosed with rheumatoid arthritis, and the medication prevented her from drinking alcohol. Once Polly quit drinking, she became clearheaded and began to hear God's voice. She describes a moment when she saw how he sees her: *Polly*, he said, *you are my daughter and I love you.*

Slowly, God began depositing the truth of her value in her heart. She received counseling to help her sort through the broken pieces of her past.

Polly had to speak about her secret. Polly had to pursue healing like her life depended on it, and that's exactly what she did. Today, Polly runs a care center for girls who aim to get out of the sex industry and find healing and purpose. "My dream," Polly says, "is for everyone to know God's extravagant love. For every woman trapped in shame to be free."

Justice is available for the man who abused Polly. God's mercy is thick, and he only has grace for the ways Polly abused herself. If she can be free—and she *is*—then so can any of us.

❀

The magazines may say that sex is a game and your body is a toy, but that is a lie from the pit of hell. It is a lie that your flesh is your value, and your flesh has no value.

God's love is so far, so wide, so deep that he will walk
the broken ground directly into the holes in your
soul. There, he will whisper into the wounds of
your heart, "You are mine."

The truth is: You have value. Your body has value. You are cherished. You are worthy, and you are loved.

You and I are God's beloved daughters and precious creations, and he will go to the end of the earth, to the heart of the blackest night, to rescue his little girls. There is no end to his love for you. It is so far, so wide, so deep that he will walk the broken and shattered ground of this sick and twisted world on a pathway directly into the holes in your soul. There, he will whisper into the wounds of your heart, "You are mine."

He says he will come and make his home in us. At one time, God lived in temples built by human hands. But since the days of Christ, your body is the temple he lives in. You are literally the Lord's house.

The Lord Speaks

Magazines are made of words and images printed on paper, which burns in the fire. The lies of the world are traps. You are walking along, believing that you are less, and you get your foot caught in a sharp-toothed snare. You fall to the ground, crying for help.

Maybe someone stole your purity, or maybe you gave it away, and for both I'm sorry. I never intended for you, my daughter, to be a convenience store. I crafted you as a holy place, my temple where I live and move and have my being.

When you or others hock the handcrafted vase of your body as if it could be up for sale, your soul gets lost with nowhere to rest. It tears my heart when my baby girls' hearts get torn. Even when they don't know it's happening, I do.

Here is my heart for you, Daughter: to turn away from the world's definition of your body and turn to me for its reflection. Through faith in my Son, you are unblemished. Unstained. Pure.

Anything that soils you in this world can be erased by the blood of Christ. You wear white in my eyes, not because of where you've been, but because of the cross.

Dedicate your body to me; lay it down on my altar, for it is already mine. I don't just want you to call me Lord. I want to be Lord of the temple of you.

Holy Ground

God is very specific when he crafts a temple. In the Old Testament, his directions to Solomon for the building of the temple were precise. Exact measurements, detailed instructions, and elaborate adornments were God's signature on the house that bore his name.

At one time, God lived in a temple built by human hands. But since the days of Christ, your body is the temple he lives in.

He crafts us much the same way. From the outside, he beautifies us. From the inside, he sanctifies us. He marks us as holy ground. On the interior of Solomon's temple, the floors were inlaid with pure gold and the walls embellished with priceless stones. When people entered the temple, they had to take off their shoes because it was holy ground.

Only the priests could enter behind the curtain once a year into the Most Holy Place, to make a sacrifice for the people's sins.

Magazines have had their time of influence, but they will pass. Only the Word will last, and its message couldn't be more opposite that of the world: "Don't you know that you yourselves are God's temple and that God's Spirit dwells in your midst?...God's temple is sacred, and you together are that temple" (1 Corinthians 3:16-17). "Do you not know your bodies are temples of the Holy Spirit, who is in you, whom you have received from God? You are not your own; you were bought at a price. Therefore honor God with your body" (1 Corinthians 6:19-20).

Our bodies are not things to be bought and sold, stolen, or given away at will. Our bodies are also not objects to be analyzed and criticized. Our bodies are tents for his Spirit to dwell in, if we allow him that place in our lives.

We always have the option to choose sin or him. He lets us pick. Too often, we choose self over heaven. We choose sickness over health. We choose sin over the goodness God wants for us.

Then we feel this darkness creep in, flooding our hearts.

We run to the temple and cry, "Lord, Lord!"

And he says to us, "Please, don't just call me Lord. Let me *be* your Lord."

Forgiven

When I first started writing my story, I relived each moment so closely that I remembered details I had shut out years prior. Writing revived old pains that became fresh and real again, and the ugliness of certain points in my life as a young woman came to the surface.

The pain manifested itself physically. I had jaw pain and skin problems, and doctors told me I had to speak of the hurt to heal from it. I saw a counselor who helped me forgive myself. That was a big step, but that was as far as I went; I stopped going, thinking I was done. But the truth is I didn't want to go deeper. I didn't want to look at my childhood or deal with all the people I was mad at deep down. I just wanted to move on.

But we are the temple of God, and he wants his house clean. So buried pain always surfaces.

Right after we moved from California to Texas, I spoke at an event for a woman named Deborah. The room was filled with businesswomen for whom I shared my story and spoke about the lies of the magazines. As I read the titles on the covers and tossed the pages to the ground, the anger in my voice boomed through the microphone, though I did not realize it at the time.

For years I had been telling my story to audiences young and old, and it seemed that no matter how proper the environment, I always shed some tears at one point. Yet that day it was not just one or two tears I could easily wipe away; this time they streamed down my face as I strained to speak.

A few months later, Deborah invited me to lunch.

"The daughter of the King is not a victim, Jen," she told me. "She is a victor. You are still angry."

"I *am* angry!" I cried in the corner booth. I was angry at so many people. I was angry at my father, my brother, and the men in the modeling industry. I was angry at models and magazines and the media at large. I was furious that my life had so many moments where I believed men had failed me. Little did I know this anger was affecting not only my ministry but all of my relationships.

After diagnosing unforgiveness as the source of my anger, Deborah told me to open my heart every day and ask the Lord to "reveal any unclean thing hidden within me." I began to pray exactly that.

Sin and light cannot coexist in God's temple. God is continually cleaning out his temple and making sure it is a fit place to shine his light. He is always overturning the unclean things of our hearts and making sure that it's not just pretty on the surface, but it's pretty inside.

Sometimes we have to go back in time to take a close look at the source of our anger to heal from it. For me, that meant going through my portfolios one last time. For others, it might be diaries or picture albums or memory books. The key to healing is releasing the past so we can walk free into the future.

Pulling all of the photos out of my portfolios and going through the stacks was an exhausting, confusing experience. Every time I had tried to sort through the pictures over the years, I could never finish organizing them. Giving up, I would shut the bin and stuff it back in the closet.

Often the photos looked fine on the surface, but in my mind I could only see the man behind the camera whom I had naïvely trusted but who turned out to be a snake. As a young woman I would pose for the cover of a decent magazine, but sometimes the client or photographer—twice my age or older—would proposition me for sex. I was totally disgusted by these men and refused their advances.

When I came home from quitting the business, my modeling pictures represented lies to me; I wanted to burn them all but didn't have the wisdom or courage to sort through them. Now, with piles of pictures all over the floor, so many years later, my heart swelled with pain and anger clogged my throat. I was so young! So naïve! Why did I still carry so much hurt in my heart?

It's much easier to put the hurt at the bottom of a box and try to forget it ever existed. But it's harder to forgive, because you have to look your offender and the offense straight in the eye. You have to face how their sin hurt you and how you hurt yourself.

My husband, Shane, helped me sort through the piles of my modeling photos and rummage through the stories of my past. God moved through him to help me do what I could never do: divide the good from the bad. Not all of my pictures represented painful times. Many didn't. Many were great adventures in beautiful places. Many were completely innocent. Most were taken with decent people. Many of the photos also represented my journey from a young girl to a woman. It was my journey, and it wasn't all bad.

With hundreds of photos scattered all over the floor, I was finally able to look at each one and weigh its worth. Had this been a negative experience? Was I demeaned? Or was this okay? I sorted the images into "keep" and "burn" piles.

Late in the night we stood in the backyard under a starry sky. Shane took a big metal canister and we filled it with the pile of photos that represented the loss of my value as a young woman. Wearing a purple silk scarf over my head, I rested beneath my husband's wing and the cloak of the starry sky; my heart knew the Lord had surfaced the unclean things in my life, and I had to face them and let them go.

Holding a large stick in his hand, Shane prayed as he stirred the burning images, poking at the hundreds of pages as they disintegrated into ash. In the hot orange flames I saw dead spirits crackle and groan. No longer would the pain other men caused me hurt the men in my life now. No longer would their abuse cause me to distrust men today. No longer would I carry bitterness in my heart like a poison.

That night, my past became a bucket of ashes. Getting rid of the guck in my heart changed things for me and Shane. For Shane, he said he saw me through the eyes of Christ: holy, without blemish, pure as the bride.

And for me, I got a new chance at life: to not walk wounded, but to walk victorious. The next morning, I felt brand new.

At one time or another, we have all held on to anger. We know we've been forgiven but still have this bitter taste in our mouth against those who hurt us. Sometimes we want to choke the life out of our offenders because in some way they cut off our air.

But the unforgiveness doesn't choke those who hurt us; it suffocates us instead. Our spirits can't be free because we are holding somebody else in prison. My anger against people in my life didn't really hold them captive; it held me.

The burning was the beginning of the *real* forgiveness that had to take place. I couldn't just say of the men, "I forgive them" and sweep my hand across the sky and forget. I had to look each hurt in the face and say, "I forgive him or her for _____." I had to march each one to the cross. And all the while, I had to face my own sin and the choices I had made. I had to take responsibility for the ways I hurt myself and others.

It started with the burning, but it was a long journey to forgiveness. God was cleaning out my temple, turning over every unclean stone at the floor of my heart and washing me from the inside out.

This cleansing tide went on for a long time. Sometimes I felt like I was never going to come up for air. But over time I realized the cleansing never really stops. It's just how God works; his whole goal is that we would be temples that shine his light, so he's always exposing the darkness there. The more we allow him, the better off we are.

Zeal for His House

After Jesus died, the temple changed from being a place people visited to encounter God to being *people*—you and me. The apostle Paul wrote, "Don't you know that you yourselves are God's temple and that God's spirit dwells in your midst?" (1 Corinthians 3:16). Jesus had an intimate relationship with the temple. If you take a close look at his interactions with the temple, you can learn a lot about the way he views you.

When he was a baby, Mary and Joseph carried him to the temple in Jerusalem to be dedicated. When we first ask Christ into our lives, it's like he is born into our "temples." He's like a baby just in the gate of our hearts. We become "baby" Christians and don't know the grown-up Jesus quite yet or the ways he wants us to grow up. But the important thing is we've invited him "into the house."

According to the Gospels, the next time we see Jesus in the temple is when he is twelve. I love this story because Mary loses track of him for three days. Honestly, it gives me comfort as a mother to know that Mary, the mother of the King of the universe, was so human that she lost him. She must have been like, "Well, he's supposed to save the world, but first I have to find him! Joseph, where is Jesus?!"

Where did they find him? In the temple. Sitting with the teachers of the law and prophets, listening, asking questions (Luke 3:46).

Over time, Christ starts to grow up in us. He takes the temperature of what's happening in our temples. He begins leaning in and listening, asking questions. *What do you think of this?* he might ask. *How do you feel about that? What do you think God thinks about it?* If we listen well, we may be amazed at his answers.

The next time we see Jesus in the temple is when he stands up to quote Isaiah 61:1-3, announcing the start of his adult ministry.

There comes a time for all of us when Jesus stands up in us, when he's ready for us to move from milk to meat. He talks to us in grown-up terms. *I came to bring you good news,* he might say. *Why are you still living like you haven't heard it? I came to bind up your broken heart; don't keep it from me, daughter. I can sew up the jagged edges. I came to free you from prison; don't lock yourself behind bars. I came to release you from darkness; why do you insist on venturing into the dark? I came to comfort you when you mourn, to bestow on you a crown of beauty instead of ashes, a spirit of joy instead of mourning, a garment of praise instead of despair. Get out of your ashes, daughter—hold your head high and look to me as I crown you mine. Lift your hands to praise me; it will lift your feet out of the net. I came to root you in me, so grow deep and branch out into the world healthy and strong!*

Sometimes Jesus stands up in us and declares why he is here, what he wants to accomplish in us, and it's up to us to stay open and realize every temple needs a Lord, and we are not the lord; we are only the house for the Lord. Only he is capable of transforming us from the inside out.

The next time we see Jesus in the temple, he takes a whip of cords and drives out the money changers, the doves, and the cattle. "Get these out of here!" he cries. "How dare you turn my Father's house into a market!" Zeal for God's house consumed him. He couldn't stand by while people turned his temple into a cheap place to sell their wares.

From the outside, he beautifies us. From the inside, he sanctifies us. He marks us as holy ground.

Jesus may decide you need a good temple-clearing too. He may come into your temple with a whip of cords and drive out the sin. He may turn over your tables, shed a spotlight on some unclean thing in you, and say, *You can't live this way anymore. You are my Father's house, and zeal for you consumes me! I love you too much to let you keep living in anger, sexual sin, jealousy, or lies. Even if it's going to hurt, I am going to drive this out of you and I will not give up on you because you are my dwelling place. I don't just want you to call me Lord; I want to be your Lord. I want to reign in the temple of you.*

Jesus taught people in the temple, healed people in the temple, and broke human rules to reach human hearts in the temple. He was whipped outside the temple courts. They put a crown of thorns on him and mocked him, right near his Father's house. The people tore his flesh by whipping him with cords of spiked steel.

When Jesus died on the cross, the curtain in the temple was torn from top to bottom and the foundations shook and crumbled. When he rose again three days later, he rebuilt that temple, and from there on out, the Bible refers to the temple as *you*.

You are the temple of the Holy Spirit. Many of us might respond, "Look, I'm not Mary, okay? I'm not holy. I've dirtied my temple. I can't be in God's presence. I'm mad at everyone in my life. I'm *not* holy."

This is where the good news sweeps in and sweeps us out, clearing our temples of the unclean things. As the truth of his Son rushes in, his light chases out the darkness.

The Word says, "Your bodies are temples of the Holy Spirit." Period. God says, *My blood makes you clean. By one sacrifice for all men for all time, you can enter into my presence. You are holy to me.* And one day he will say to you, *Daughter, I want to do some miracles through the temple of you. Open your gates so I can shine.*

The Temple Gate Called Beautiful

They are so beautiful, I thought to myself as I laid my tired head on my husband's lap and gazed at the TV. He stroked my frizzy, kinky hair in silence, while the usual battle raged in this fragile head of mine.

It was the Oscars, and the beautiful people had come out to receive their applause. The hems of their long, flowing gowns swished as the images of ideal women sashayed down the red carpet. They looked so *perfect,* and I felt so *not.*

As the stars twirled and smiled over their shoulders as if they had stepped out of a dream, I thought, *I'll never look like them. What is beautiful to you, God?* I begged to know.

Then one day I came across the story of the temple gate called Beautiful (Acts 3:1-10). In the story, the disciples Peter and John are on their way to an afternoon prayer meeting when they see a man begging in front of the temple gate. The man, lame from birth, is carried every day to the temple gate to beg. When he sees Peter and John, he puts out his cup, expecting to get something from them. But the disciples look straight into his eyes.

Please don't just call me Lord. Let me *be* your Lord.

This reminds me of the people I met in the park in Germany. They weren't too busy to look in the eyes of a lost and hurting girl. They were average-looking—you wouldn't see them on the red carpet. But they stopped for me and cared about me. They didn't just flip a coin into my empty cup. They gave me water that would fill it forever.

Peter says to the beggar, "Silver or gold I do not have, but what I do have I give you. In the name of Jesus Christ of Nazareth, walk." Then Peter reaches out his hand and helps the beggar to his feet.

After a lifetime of paralysis the man's ankles become miraculously strong and he jumps to his feet, praising God. Holding on to Peter and John, he goes into the temple courts, shouting that a miracle has occurred. Everyone recognizes the beggar and it causes a huge uproar.

There was a time in my life when I was like the beggar at the temple gate, crippled and empty and looking for something to fill me. But today I get to be more like Peter and John, telling others about Jesus, teaching in the temple, proclaiming miracles and causing a stir. It all started with people who took the time to look into my eyes and offer me Jesus.

Jesus is the gate. You are the temple. His Spirit within you is beautiful.

Don't be in such a rush that you can't see the hurting people all around you. Stop for them, look directly at them, give them what you've got. Reach out and touch others. Offer them hope that they too can be healed.

Beauty to God isn't what he sees on the red carpet. Beauty to God is beheld in the red blood of his Son, in the crimson core of your heart.

Be who you are made to be—a temple gate called Beautiful.

7   The Fourth Lie:

You Are the Mask You Wear

Unmasked, we are prettiest.

The Most Beautiful Woman in the World

Last year, *People* magazine revealed its "Most Beautiful Woman in the World," her image selling the cover while we saw her skin, hair, clothes, and body plastered all over television, in music videos, reality TV, magazines, you name it. The magazine came out right at the time her marriage fell apart and divorce proceedings began. I bring this up not with judgment for her but with empathy. Divorce can be horrible. It is the shattering not only of promises but of dreams and futures.

Ignoring this truth, the media applauded the Most Beautiful Woman in the World with lots of follow-up articles and TV shows revealing how fantastic she looked while going through her divorce. The media subtly lets us know, "Women can break up their marriages and look fab doing it!" Or even worse, "Why do you look so bad? What's the big deal if your family falls apart?"

God's brushstrokes of beauty are vast and varied.

If you have experienced divorce, you know it can rip people's hearts, sometimes to shreds. The breakup of a family is tragic, and it's a lie to think that anyone can look fabulous while enduring it. It's a complete masquerade.

Masks like that scare me. I know what it's like to pretend things are okay when they are not. It's painful, and it's real. In no way am I surprised when I open a tabloid and see the page entitled "Divorce of the Week." There we see yet another hurting star—the same one listed on a later page as one of the "fashionistas" we should imitate.

What is worth imitating? A flawless body or a successful marriage? What is beautiful? Fabulous makeup and a glittering gown or lasting love and a happy family?

The "curse of the Oscar" is infamous in Hollywood; from the years 2001 to 2010, seven winners for Best Actress experienced the heartbreak of their marriages shattering at the time they won the Oscar. As they unveiled their exquisite gowns and rich adornments, dripped in costly fabric and pricey jewels, the primary relationship in their life shattered, and their children were left with the fallout.

So we are left with this question: What is beautiful? What is worth applauding? What is stellar and amazing and victorious for women? Is it really about the accomplishment, the trophy, the stage, the applause? Or is beauty something no one sees? Is allure more about the way we treat our families at the end of the day, beauty more about the way we talk to our best friends, and radiance all about where we look for guidance?

Surely, we cannot just be as pretty as the picture we present.

The Masquerade

As a kid I was fascinated by Michael Jackson. I read every available biography about him and tacked his posters on my bedroom walls. I kept scrapbooks of all the magazine articles written about him. I even had a doll that looked just like Michael.

Michael was the self-proclaimed king of pop—on the outside, talented, famous, and wealthy. He garnered the attention of millions as paparazzi clamored to capture his every move. Everywhere he went, Michael was a showstopper. People were literally obsessed with him and exalted him like a god.

But behind the façade, he was lonely, vulnerable, and perhaps lost.

Despite his fame, his soul suffered. His inner torment manifested itself publicly in his failed efforts to achieve what he thought was the perfect face. The more he permitted surgeons to carve his nose, the less handsome he looked. His journey had a horrible destination: In search of perfect beauty, he became deformed.

Michael missed the truth that all too many women and girls miss: They are the manifestation of beauty in the first place. When Michael died, it saddened me to know he didn't see himself through his Creator's eyes; he was a prisoner behind the mask.

Masks have a way of falling out of place, and when we peek behind them, the interior world doesn't always match the surface.

We can list the stars for which this has been true—Marilyn Monroe, Whitney Houston, and others. Today's stars are all too similar.

Hannah Montana is the sad but true classic picture of the world's values. The world adored her innocence and applauded her beauty and talent, even making costumes for little girls to dress up to be just like her. Now, the girl who played Hannah has broken out of that shell. But paparazzi and fans are right on her footsteps, capturing, following, and imitating her every move. The conclusion? Look pretty outside, even when sickness is bubbling beneath the surface. Make yourself as unholy as possible, and people will worship the *image* of what is beautiful instead of what is *truly* beautiful.

Glamour is an illusion. Pretty outside doesn't mean pretty inside. Just because something looks good doesn't mean it *is* good. What we see in pictures and on TV is often not true to life. Riches don't bring true, lasting joy, fame doesn't promise real fulfillment, and talent doesn't guarantee love or happiness.

Unmasking our pain is the beginning of healing.

One of the most tragic lies in our world is *You are the mask you wear*. If we are not pinpointing our identity on men, mirrors, or magazines, we focus on the image we project. We spend more time and energy on the outward image than making sure our hearts are beautiful too.

The world is obsessed with masks, applauding and even worshipping the beautiful people regardless of the often sick states of their private worlds.

Most young, wealthy stars fall. Most rebel against the pressure to be perfect. Most kick and scream by way of drinking or drugs or sexual exploitation. Most play the rebel, at least for a while. Behavior and choices in our world don't define beauty; image does. So the world keeps analyzing the stars' gowns, shoes, purses, hair, makeup, bodies, lovers, and latest gimmicks, regardless of whether their private lives are worthy of imitation.

The Bible teaches that when we worship images of people instead of our Creator, our hearts become filled with darkness (Romans 1:21-22). Why are so many girls of this generation cutting themselves? Why are so many turning on their own bodies through drugs, alcohol, food, and sex?

Images of the media have turned our gaze away from our Lord. Instead of focusing on him for our beauty and value, we focus on other women. The media sculpts a very narrow definition of beauty and worth. God's brushstrokes of beauty are vast and varied; beauty to him is all about the heart.

But it's always easier to focus on what we *can* see than on what we *can't* see. In this world, the stars are exalted like gods. We are supposed to esteem their light and approve of their accomplishments, even if there is a rotting mess beneath the exterior. But the more we focus on the stars, the worse we feel. We begin to hear lies like, *You are not enough. You should be more.*

Deep down, every girl wants to shine. Every girl wants to be pretty in light of her imperfections. And every girl wants someone to see beyond her exterior shell, peer into her heart, and accept her truth, whatever it may be.

Unmasked

The first high school girls' event I spoke at was called "Unmasked." I was asked to speak at this event during my season of "unmasking," battling cystic acne by fasting from the mirror.

When I arrived at the event, the girls were wearing matching bright blue shirts. They streamed into the building hugging their pillows and toting their overnight bags, huge smiles on their faces. They were probably excited that a former model was coming to speak to them. Or maybe they were excited to get out of the house for a huge sleepover, which is the best part. I *love* sleepovers!

On Friday night, behind the podium, I followed a detailed outline of my story. I wasn't a skilled speaker, but I presented my heart on a platter and gave the girls everything I had. That night they went back to the host homes and poured out their own stories with each other. Telling my truth inspired them to tell theirs too.

The next morning, something amazing happened. As I spoke of my struggles with image and value, their struggles surfaced: eating disorders, the pain of their parents' divorces, their mothers' obsessions with appearance, rejection at school. At times they laughed; at times they cried and came to support each other at the altar, where they had the opportunity to trade in the lies they'd believed for the truth of how they looked in God's eyes.

I fell in love with the girls—the skinny blondies, the tough athletes, the overweight beauties. I loved the misfits, the cheerleaders, the scholars, the dreamers. But my heart especially wrapped around the lonely and broken ones who didn't feel loved or precious —the ones who had believed they were less and needed someone to believe they were more.

Unmasking our pain is the beginning of healing. Then there is a point when we stop looking at our pasts and ourselves and choose to look outward. Choosing to help others from the center of our own experience completes our healing and brings us full circle. There is nothing more satisfying than taking our past and turning it into purpose, inspiring a better future for the girl coming up the road behind us.

❧

Women and girls hide behind masks for several reasons. Sometimes they are afraid of getting hurt, so their mask becomes a wall protecting them from a tough world. Sometimes their parents teach them to wear masks, making everything look good when it's not. Other times a mask is a way for a woman to look beautiful on the outside when she doesn't know who she is inside. Deeper still, masks hide our secrets.

It's dark behind a mask, and hard to see. Taking off the masks and setting them down is the beginning of our truth, and truth sets us free. When I shed my masks and got real about what my life in the modeling industry was like, it wasn't pretty at first. But over time, being honest about my experiences helped me heal from them. When women get honest and get real, they heal. And when women heal, they can be lights for people around them.

Nothing is more satisfying than turning
your past into purpose.

These days I speak in schools. Before I arrive, I try to talk to the counselor. If anyone knows what goes on behind the masks of junior high and high school girls, she does. Sometimes my heart hurts when I get off the phone with her. I find out girls are skipping lunch to be skinnier. Girls are getting weird about food. Girls are dressing promiscuously, yet it's tough to do much about it since they are following their mothers' examples. Girls are sharing their bodies with boys, posting sexy images of themselves, harassing each other or cyberbullying. Girls are sometimes overtly jealous and hateful. Some girls are abused. Others are criticized for their weight or grades. Girls are trying to be the perfect athlete to please Mom and Dad. Girls are cracking under the pressure to perform. Girls—even in junior high—are cutting…or trying to recover from the pain of a friend who committed suicide.

And you've called me? I think. *Who am I?* I am nothing but a girl who raised her hand one day, and said, "Here I am. Send me!" (Isaiah 6:8).

But even with all these issues, many of the girls of this generation are making great choices and going great places. The vast majority are devoted friends. They help each other tell the truth and get help when needed; they believe in each other and inspire each other to believe the best of themselves. Lots of girls are hard workers and have a destiny in mind. Many understand that perfection isn't the goal and realize success is an inside job. Lots of girls want to make huge differences in the world, and they will.

You have all the opportunity in the world to be great. Everything you need for a full life is accessible to you. You are the wonder of the world—the new generation—and you can imprint this world with faith, love, and true beauty.

Yet with all your opportunity and potential, the world will no doubt try to rob your innocence, warp your sexuality, burden your heart, and steal your destiny. What can we do about suicide pacts and cutting and abuse? What can we do about girls who hate their bodies and hate their fathers and hate themselves? All we can do is look to God and ask for help. All we can do is take off our masks and show other girls we are loved for who we are beneath the surface. And we can live our message when no one's looking.

Sometimes when I speak in the schools, I shock the girls by taking out a porcelain mask and smashing it with a great big hammer. The hammer's strike and broken pieces thrill them.

When the girls settle down, a wave of relief washes over their faces. They learn that masks hide their real beauty instead of revealing it. I tell them the truth: They are worth more than jealousy, bullying, and sexting. They possess beauty, worth, and purpose.

It's up to you to choose: Live like you are less or live like you are more.

Afterward, the girls pour forward. Their stories have gotten knocked loose and surfaced. Like a river whose dam breaks, after the program they are either too broken up to speak or so broken their truths spill. It's such a release for them. They usually have to rush off to class before the tardy bell rings, and I find myself longing for more time with them. I want to know they heard me. I want to prevent them from making the same mistakes I did. I want to save each last girl.

When women get honest and get real, they heal.

But I can't. Saving them isn't up to me. It never was. What is up to me, and what is up to you, is to make yourself available, wherever you are. There's a girl coming up the road behind you who needs to know your story, who needs to hear your truth, and who needs your faith like an anchor for the storm.

Getting Real

Every Disney princess had an evil enemy who was after her heart. She rightly possessed the crown as an inheritance from the king; she had the potential to rule and reign in the land. But there was always an evil force trying to steal her crown from her. Whether it was Maleficent, the Mistress of All Evil, devising a plan to injure and silence Sleeping Beauty; the evil stepsisters locking Cinderella in her room; the Evil Queen devising a scheme to kill Snow White; or Ursula the Sea Witch determined to rob Ariel of her exquisite voice, there was always an enemy plotting to destroy the princess. If the enemy could kill her, or at least silence her, he could devour her light and destroy the potential of her good influence.

The evil one is always dark and his eyes are filled with fury. He wants to keep the girl trapped in darkness where he is. He wants to mute her so she cannot bless the world with her beauty. He wants to cover her with a mask and steal her voice, telling her she is unworthy, unloved, and powerless.

I am all too familiar with this enemy and his lies. At one time he had me muted, sleeping in a depression from which I could hardly wake. At first, my mask-wearing looked pretty. But then, the masks held me captive because what people saw on the outside was a lie. It became so dark, I considered suicide. I injured myself. I allowed others to abuse me and speak for me. There were heavy chains around my soul hidden beneath a perfect mask.

And then the King who sees behind our masks roused me from my slumber and told me I was made for more. He unlocked my chains, unleashed my lies, and released truth to pour into my heart like sunlight.

When I left the modeling industry, I ran fast and furious. Although it offered travel, money, and prestige, I had come to loathe the masquerade. I had seen too many hurting girls behind the pristine façades; too many lost, wandering souls trapped behind demands of perfection. I too had become a prisoner to the shell. If I was hurting, it wasn't allowed to show; I just had to buck up and be pretty. If I felt degraded or disregarded or disgusted, I had to smile and make nice. I had to stuff down my emotions to the point that I became sick. Everything about it went against the grain of my soul's fabric.

Over the years I have found that women and girls across the board hate masks. We are repelled by them yet often trapped behind them. We are afraid to speak the truth and say what hurts; we fear rejection, blame, and shame. Yet we must push through our fears and seek the help we need. We simply cannot buy into the media's images of perfect beauty that make drama look glamorous, rebellion look appealing, and cover-ups the norm.

❧

Women and girls who do not speak openly of their pain are hard to heal. For me personally, it took years to tell the truth of my experience. But when I did, the journey of healing began.

In his life on earth, Jesus was more interested in people who took off the mask than people who made themselves look good. The more vulnerable a woman was, the more honest about her story, the more humble about her need for him, the more courageous she was in not following the crowd but pursuing him instead, the more beautiful he considered her to be. Jesus called mask-wearers "whitewashed tombs," who looked good and plastic on the outside but on the inside were full of death and destruction.

When we wear a mask—making it look good when in truth it's not good—it becomes death to us. By not being real about our pain, we instead turn inward, harming ourselves. When girls believe the lie that they do not have a voice, they can desire to hurt themselves as a way to release the emotional agony. But telling the truth is the first relief, and continuing to tell it ushers in healing. As Jesus said, "The truth will set you free."

You are the wonder of the world, and you can imprint
this world with faith, love, and true beauty.

When we hurt, God knows the source of our pain and can touch the place only he knows will heal it. He'd rather we crack open a perfume bottle and pour out every ounce of our souls than stand around looking pretty to everybody else, pretending we don't need a Savior.

When we take off our masks, there is nothing separating us from God. We are barefaced and can face our one true mirror. So here's my question: When we are alone with God and he shows us the ugliness of our own sin, will we have the courage to face it and own it? Will we have the courage to shatter our masks in a thousand pieces on the ground, believing that in his eyes we are loved and accepted and changed for the better? Will we have the courage to believe beauty is what God sees when our hearts are bare and we are facing him, and him only? Will we walk away knowing that beauty is honesty?

You are more than the mask you wear, and when you are honest about what lies beneath the surface, freedom, healing, and purpose wash the shore of your soul. God's territory is light; God's language is truth. When you walk in the light, you leave the earth imprinted with your realness and beautified by your honesty, and others are inspired to follow your steps. Because you walk in the light, others will also want this unmasking, where all is real, all is well, and all is made whole.

8 The Fourth Truth:

You Are a Shining Light

You are the light of the world.
MATTHEW 5:14

The Morning Star Speaks

asks are shells, a protective covering for a tender core, the outer armor guarding the tender soul. Masks are not always bad. Sometimes people have to put on the face and fake it 'til they make it; it's a mode of combat in a hard world. My daughters get thick-skinned from battle; it's natural and can be good.

What's not good is falsehood. Pretending leads to sorrow. Lies get buried beneath the surface, pain gets masked, and no one heals. Transparency is beautiful; people are attracted by it. I never had to be fake because I knew who I was and whose I was. My identity was my truth; this freed me to share my truth without reservation.

There used to be a curtain in the temple that separated people from entering my presence, but it tore when I died on the cross. You can pass through the curtain now. You can come to me with an unmasked face.

I love your truth, but I want it whole.

For just a moment on the mountain, I showed my closest friends my whole truth—all that I am on the inside. Shedding the cloak of my humanity, I allowed my glory to turn inside out. It was so dazzling that they fell over speechless. My honesty was too much for them.

But most of the time I didn't tell people I was God; I just loved them like he does. People were drawn to me because of the flickering flame I held within—it wasn't my good looks or great talent! I never sought fame. I came to serve. People fell in love with my heart.

Lucifer, on the other hand, loved the outside of things. He took great pride in his good looks and he wanted to be worshipped for his wealth, wisdom, and beauty. He aspired to be a star above all stars, even calling himself the son of the dawn. But no matter how good he looked on the outside, his pride made him the ugliest beast.

People worship the movie stars and their hearts grow dark. When you worship me, I pour my light into you.

And the beauty I give lasts.

All fall short of the glory of God. None of us can go up to a mountain like Jesus did and turn ourselves inside out, blazing white. But people do have a way of making men into gods.

The Bible teaches when we worship images of people, our foolish hearts darken. I know this because I have done this. I did it in the modeling industry (where I was constantly compared to other women) and I've done it in my adult life, where I begin to think, "If only I were as pretty as her, then…"

As soon as we catch ourselves gazing for too long at what other women have, we have to stop. Turn our hearts to Jesus. He is the Star. He is the light. He is the maker of our bodies and souls and the filler of our cups. He solidifies us. As the potter, only he can smooth the cracks in us, and only he can fill us to overflowing. Trying to be more like someone else will never make us overflow.

Every woman has her season of glory. But as Isaiah says, like a flower, she will bloom and then she will pass. Our fate is the same: We turn to dust and our spirits return to God. When a woman passes her time of glory—whether she is a movie star, a teacher, a grandmother, or a friend—she fades like a flower and dies. Why did we waste our time making her into a god, a mirror by which we define beauty?

The best we can do when we see a beautiful woman (and by beautiful I mean *faithful, steadfast, loving, kind, gentle, peaceful,* and *warm*) is to imitate her character qualities and ask God to form them in us.

So no matter how much you think other women or girls look perfect, do not try to conform to their image. God made you great. You have your own unique beauty and worth and contribution to make to the world—and that's yours alone.

When Jesus died, he tore down the curtain in the temple. When you pass through the curtain now and take off your mask, in his presence, he will transform you to be more like him. That's the goal: to be more like *him.* That, my friend, is no mask. That's beautiful, inside and out.

Some stars basking in the limelight of the world's biggest stages are also shining brilliant lights in kids' hospital rooms. Some stars are walking the war-torn areas of the world, carrying water and digging wells. Some are carrying babies right out of the darkest, most hopeless settings and giving them homes where love reigns. Some of the movie stars' marriages are surviving and thriving.

Everyone is inspired when athletes and musicians and actresses impact the world with uncomplicated love. We appreciate it when they understand that to whom much is given, much is expected. Deep down we all realize that real stars wash dirty feet and touch the sick and fight for their marriages and children.

Beauty begins in the heart, and it spills out in our words, attitudes, and behavior.

Beauty begins at home, where there are no makeup artists, no lighting specialists, and no trophies for a job well done. Because the world emphasizes image over reality, outward success over family life, and money over marriage, many girls of this generation might believe that being a light to the world means shining their light *outside the home* rather than shining their light *within it.*

This issue is very close to my heart. Over a season of my life, I started believing that being a light to the world meant the world outside these walls where my family lives. Now I am convinced that being radiant is what happens when no one is looking and no one is applauding.

The Covering

My very first opportunity to share my testimony on television ended badly. I flew to Nashville, recorded a TV show, and on my way back, missed my connecting flight due to a fog delay. I had to take a different route home, so when I arrived at the wrong airport, my husband called a cab to drive me two and a half hours to the airport where my car was. When I got to that tiny little airport at three in the morning, it was closed down for the night. Then I realized I didn't have my car keys! I had slipped them into the bag that I had checked back in Nashville.

In God's eyes, it's who we are when
no one's looking that matters.

Standing in an empty airport, looking out at an empty parking lot filled with fog, I tried to figure out what to do on my own. I hoped and prayed my bag was in the locked airline storage room, but there was no one at the airport but the cleaning crew.

I began praying for an angel to come and help me.

The next thing I know, I see this woman in an American Airlines uniform, a big rack of keys hanging on her belt loop. A miracle! I tell her my issue—I've lost my bag and have no way to get home. We lived hours away up a steep mountain in the fog, and my husband was at home with our sleeping children.

The lady lets me into the baggage room and my bag is not there. Crying, I call my husband, and he tries to tell me what to do to get home. But I think I know a better way, so I disagree with him and begin to argue.

The woman, who has clear blue eyes, a beautiful face, and a long silver braid, taps me on the shoulder. "Excuse me," she says respectfully. "I need to tell you something. Can you tell him to hold on just a moment?" Her eyes are gentle but firm.

I excuse myself from Shane and press the receiver to my chest so he can't hear me.

"Are you a believer?" she asks.

"Yes," I say.

"I thought so. God wants me to tell you something."

"Yes?"

"You need to listen to your husband. He is your spiritual covering," she says, making a motion like she is outlining an umbrella above her head. "God will speak through him to you. I can explain this more later, but for now, just do whatever he tells you. Do *not* argue with him."

"Okay…" I say, somewhat in disbelief, and I agree to Shane's plan to get me home.

When I get off the phone, she tells me that if I ever go out of my husband's covering, it will be like jutting out into a rainstorm instead of staying under the safety of his umbrella. If I argue and disagree with him, there will be angst and turmoil, she tells me. Trust your husband's covering, she says. God will speak through him. Listening to his voice will be a protection for you.

I nod my head like I understand. But it would take tragedy and trials and lots of disagreements, years later, for me to really understand it.

Broken

Around the time I began telling my story, I began to feel like my life was being ripped apart at the seams. One might say it was the devil.

One might say it was pride on my part. Or one might say it's just that life is hard, and we all hit storms.

An international organization that provides support for third-world children contacted me to see if I would become their representative. It sounded like a wonderful idea to me. They asked if I could join them on a trip to an impoverished area in South America so I could see the work they were doing in the poorest parts of the world. I was pregnant with our third child, Samuel, at the time, so we checked with our doctor and he was fine with the trip.

The organization planned to bring a cameraman to take pictures of me caring for the hungry so that I could come back to the States and get more people to care. Usually my husband is very supportive of my ministry activities, but he was hesitant about this one, saying he detected pride in my voice when I talked about it. Foolishly, I dismissed his concern. We sought advice, received encouragement to go, and decided to take the trip.

A few days before the plane was to take off, we went to get immunized. The nurse told us she could not vaccinate me because of my pregnancy. She also cautioned me not to go to this area of the world while pregnant; she said the risk of contracting diseases was too high and if that happened, I could harm or lose the baby.

With less than 48 hours before our plane took off, I called the organization, who assured me we would not be in diseased territory and all the food and water would be safe. But my husband didn't feel good about it and tried to get me to see it wasn't worth the risk. Forgetting what the woman in the airport had told me, I felt such a strong obligation to the organization that I argued and disagreed with my husband.

I called my mentor, Devi, who travels all around the world. She told me that if my husband didn't agree with it, the answer was no…and that was it.

"Liberation through submission," she said in her sweet, gentle voice. That sounded weird! How could going against what I wanted to do be freeing? I had a very strong independent streak rooted in traveling around the world by myself as a young woman. My rebellious streak was so strong as a teen that I had a bumper sticker on my car that read

"Question Authority!" As a child, I was not raised with concepts like submission, obedience, or headship. When I got older, I became my own master. I did my own thing, I made my own decisions, and I thought I was the ruler of my own destiny.

Give me your heart, Jesus,
because your heart is beautiful.

My husband, on the other hand, grew up in the South, where women honored their husband's voices and men protected their families. So fiercely independent me went up against my fiercely protective husband, and the battle ensued.

I should go to South America and look at the suffering! I thought. *I should believe a faithful God will protect me! It is my purpose to be a light to the world!* Somehow, I was under the impression that feeding the hungry children of the world was more important than protecting the one in my own belly, and more important than the man who puts food on my plate every night.

Maybe you can relate. Maybe you sometimes think you know better than your "covering"—your parents, guardians, or pastors. Maybe you have wanted to go your own way despite their warnings and advice. Maybe you don't really believe God speaks through your covering, so you question them all the time. That was me in this case.

On a pure note, I have been to the third world and I have seen the suffering. I truly did want to help impoverished people, but the question was whether God was calling me to do that or not. And if I had remembered what the woman in the airport had said, the answer would be no—God wasn't calling me to do that at this time because my husband, who rarely says no to me, was saying no.

I wasn't in line with what God wanted. I was putting my ambitions in the outer world above the people in my inner world.

The Bible teaches that a house divided cannot stand. The father is the head of the home, and when his voice is dishonored, nothing good will come of it. In a marriage, the man is the head. Someone has to lead. Someone has to follow. A body cannot have two heads. One person cannot pull one way while the other pulls the other way. It simply doesn't work.

It took my family being torn apart by my independent, stubborn ways for me to realize that honoring my husband's voice was the most important thing I could do to honor God. If you are still under the headship of your father, the same is true. A house divided will not stand. You cannot disrespect his voice and flourish.

In the midst of my arguing with my husband, tragedy struck. Due to the distractions of the argument, I did not know our precious dog was suffering. She died a sudden and horrible death. It broke the whole family's heart and knocked me to my knees.

God's will was done: I did not go on my trip to South America. But my children's hearts were broken and my husband was shattered because I did not listen to him. Why hadn't I just listened to him in the first place, when he didn't feel the trip was a good idea? Why was I so bent on running the show? Why did I think what other people thought was more important than what my husband thought? You can ask these same questions of yourself when it comes to your father's voice. The best way to honor the King is to respect the king in your own home.

It was before dawn when I fell to my face in a mess of tears. My Bible, falling apart at the seams, lay open before me. Begging God to speak, I opened the Word and found that a chunk from the book of Isaiah had fallen out. The words leaped out at me: "Put your house in order" (Isaiah 38:1).

The words could not have been more true. My house was out of order. I was trying to be the head. I was trying to lead. I was more interested in what I wanted than what my husband wanted, and I was putting public ministry above private peace.

The woman in the airport told me my husband was my covering—as your parents are yours—and that I wasn't to argue with him, that God would speak through him. Going outside of your parents' covering, against their blessing, will cause nothing but pain.

Every time I have argued with my husband, all I have felt is turmoil and angst. And every day that I have trusted his covering and quietly rested underneath the umbrella of who he is, I have felt peace and security. Every day.

Coming under your father's umbrella—and someday, your husband's—means holding his voice high even when you don't like what he is saying. It means putting your family first and making choices that only bless them.

We are lit by Jesus,
and he shines through all our cracks.

God does things opposite from the world. In the world, public achievement, the stage, the trophy, the lights-camera-action is what it's all about. But in God's eyes, it's who we are when no one's looking that matters. It's the girl who is humbly able to honor her parents and those in authority over her who flourishes like a tree. She bears good fruit because she knows where her sun and shade come from—she knows her covering is a blessing, and God will provide for her through them.

God lifts the humble, and the proud he lays low. And he doesn't lift us because we revel in the limelight. He lifts us because we *are* the light.

❧

Now, you aren't married yet. But I am sharing this with you in hopes that you can walk into marriage or steer the early years of your marriage with this understanding: Beauty begins at home, and honoring your husband's voice (as long as he is not leading you into sin) is essential. What he feels, what he needs, and what he sees matters more than what the world says is important.

Submission is not humiliating; it is *humility*, and there is a big difference. Humility is lifting others high, and it is realizing that through your parents, and one day through your husband, God gives you an umbrella of protection, wisdom, and guidance that you can trust. Even when you think your parents are wrong, honor them, and please, don't blame them if they make a mistake. Honor them anyway, and God will bless your heart.

I wish I had understood this verse *before* I started my marriage: "Do everything without grumbling or arguing, so that you may become blameless and pure, children of God without fault in a crooked and depraved generation. Then you will shine among them like stars in the sky" (Philippians 2:14-15). Other translations tell us that we are without blemish when we don't second-guess and we don't bicker.

Isn't it funny that the Word tells us that being without blemish or spot has to do with our *attitudes,* not our skin? In the world's eyes, being without blemish means you have clear skin—it has nothing to do with complaining or arguing! But the Word says we are a breath of fresh air when we don't second-guess or bicker. Bickering is so ugly— and anyone with clear skin can bicker!

It's so easy to complain, argue, roll our eyes, and be defiant. But to be a star in the eyes of God, we do things from a place of love and gratitude, without arguing and without complaining. We win people not by our outfits, our hair-dos, our makeup and our jewels; we win them by our hearts and our spirits. From there, we can adorn ourselves beautifully, and we are beautiful inside and out.

Over the course of the few years following our dog's death, the storms didn't let up for us. There was a lot of turmoil in our home life. I went out and spoke on the stage the things I know in my heart are true—that women's real beauty comes from the gentle and quiet spirit that is so powerful to God—but at home, I found it very challenging to tap into that spirit. All of us can become contentious, argumentative, and bitter. We try to "be better," but we can't do it on my own.

Many times, instead of fixing our eyes on Jesus we fix our eyes on the trials, circumstances, and people involved, as well as the ways we aren't good enough and our lives aren't perfect.

Like Peter sinking in the water the moment he took his eyes off Christ, when we fear and doubt, we fall. Our light gets washed away.

The more you look at something, the more you reflect it. So the more we look at what is wrong with our situation and everyone in it, the more we reflect the mess.

But the Bible says those who look to God are radiant.

The Light of the World

The first clue that pointed to the Messiah was a star in the sky. When he came to earth, he said, "I am the light of the world." And even now, heaven needs no lamp; he is the lamp. He doesn't tell us we become beautiful by masking our pain. He says we become beautiful by entering into the quiet and restful place of his presence and baring our hearts. There, he heals us. There, he forgives us. There, he receives us. And there, even when it feels like the carpet's gotten swept out from underneath us, he transforms us to be brighter and more beautiful, more and more like him.

Matthew 5:14 says, "You are the light of the world." Jesus doesn't say, you will *become* a light when you do this good thing or go to that place. He doesn't say, you will *become* a light when you act this way or that way. He says, "You *are* the light."

We always see who we are in the reflection of who he is, and our light is not defined by the mistakes we've made or the achievements we've stacked up. Our light is defined by our faith in him, and through us, he shines.

Jesus says, "A city set on a hill cannot be hidden. Nor do people light a lamp and put it under a basket, but on a stand, and it gives light to all in the house. In the same way, let your light shine before others, so that they may see your good works and give glory to your Father who is in heaven" (Matthew 5:14-16 ESV).

At one time, I did a great job "shining" for people outside my home; but I didn't do a good job shining for the people in it. Why? Maybe because it's easier to look good outside the home than it is to shine inside. But I had to decide which one mattered more to me.

I had to stop looking at people and circumstances and lay myself down to God and say, "I want to be like you; I want to reflect your faith, your hope, your love—not just to the world, but to the people up close and personal in my own kitchen, living room, and bedroom…and I want to do that with all my heart, more than I want to look good to people outside my house."

It started with early morning times praying to God. Opening the Word again as if I'd never read it before. Realizing I couldn't be a good "city on a hill," shining a light for the whole wide world, without turning on my own lamp at home.

A lamp in a home is a comfort. It means *Jesus is here*—inside my heart, inside my home. Jesus's light is kind and gentle. It is full of goodness and love. It is not afraid to confront sin, or expose it, but it is not rude in its ways. It is filled with hope and strength and desires to build others up and not tear them down. It attracts people because it lights up the dark, and people are comforted by its presence.

The good news is that we are more than the mistakes we've made and more than the mistakes we will make. We don't need to hang our heads about how imperfect we are—that only douses our light. We can look up at God and say: "You are perfect. You are beautiful. Reflect your light on me, Jesus, you who suffered; you who triumphed; you who fixed your eyes on God all the way to the cross. Jesus, reflect your heart on mine; give me your heart Jesus, because your heart is beautiful."

It's not about putting on a mask and making it look pretty; it's about asking the master makeup artist to come in and paint our hearts with his perfect brushstrokes—and the cool thing is, he airbrushes our pasts for us.

Shining his light is about letting him fill us up, letting him guide us, and being there when the people who we love come home from a long hard day in the crazy world. Love is here. Comfort is here. Food is here. Compassion is here. We will not judge others; we will forgive. We will not hold on to bitterness or jealousy or spite or blame; we will dig those things out at the root so that the soil of our hearts is clean and fresh. It's up to us to water our hearts with the peace of his presence. It's up to us to focus on the sunlight so that joy sprouts and grows; and it's up to us to imitate the Master's love.

> Everywhere we go, we splash faith.
> We splash hope. We splash love.
> We splash light on someone's darkest day.

And for those who live within our walls? It's up to us to let them know by our actions that they are more important than anything that goes on outside the home. We have the power within us, the power that raised Jesus from the dead, to call out the light in them and help them shine bright. We are lit by Jesus, and he shines through all our cracks.

Radiant

I am surrounded by radiant women—not women who have airbrushed faces, but women who have the brushstrokes of God all over their hearts and lives. Women who have allowed God to paint the pictures of their lives as he sees fit, who have laid down the canvas of themselves and let him create the picture of what's beautiful.

Sounds easy, but it's not. These are women who have endured storms as hard as can be imagined. They have lost children; they have lost husbands; they have lost breasts and hair and daughters and grandchildren. Some of their families have collapsed in a heap of rubble and they have found the diamond in the rough of it. In fact, they *became* the diamond in the rough of it. In the worst of circumstances, they came out shining like a jewel.

How? They navigated the storms by keeping their gaze fixed not on the storm, but on the Son at the horizon.

Fix your eyes on Jesus.

Fix your eyes *not* on people, *not* on the trial, but on the Bright Morning Star. He is the radiance of God's glory and the light of heaven.

He makes all things beautiful. He is good, always, and he always brings a rainbow from your storm. He tells us to root ourselves in his Word and meditate on it. Meditate on the good. The lovely. The positive.

The more you focus on something, the more you will reflect it.

That is my hope and my prayer for you and for me: that as he is the light, so are we. At home. Abroad. Everywhere we go, everywhere we turn, we splash faith. We splash hope. We splash love. We splash light on someone's darkest day.

9 The Fifth Lie:

You Are Mastered by the Media

The screen is a very bad mirror.

The Most High Speaks

The media is a vehicle, as a car is a vehicle. A vehicle can be safe and get you where you want to go. But a vehicle can also be used to destroy. Accidents can happen. Kids can drive too fast, not realizing the effect of their actions. Mothers can get distracted by the children in the backseat and not see the road in front of them. People can get drunk or high or too tired and drive into a ditch and die. People can crash into others, destroying lives.

The media is like a vehicle.

Drive carefully.

Use with caution.

The slightest turn can easily run you off the road.

Fix your eyes straight ahead. Do not turn to the right or the left. Keep your eye on the goal and remember: You are the master of the vehicle; your hands are on the steering wheel. You control it. It doesn't control you.

If you ever feel like any source of media is controlling you, take your foot off the gas, pull to the side, put it in park, and get out of the car. In other words, turn off the switch, shut down the screen, and walk away. If the gravitational pull on that screen is stronger than the one you have to your loved ones, to me, and to my calling on your life, toss the screen. Remove

even the remote possibility of it tormenting you. If you ask me, I'll help you
put guards in place to make sure you know how to drive the vehicle.

You are the master of the media; don't let it master you.

The screens are everywhere. Before we talk about how detrimental they can be, we've got to say how great they are. I love being able to text simple notes to our daughter on her phone or watch funny videos of our sons. In fact, when I don't know which screw to buy at the hardware store, I just send my husband a picture and he tells me! I barely know what to do without looking at my phone calendar each day, and throughout the writing of this book, my friends have encouraged me via text messages. I love a great movie, am crazy about my Bible software program, and seriously appreciate the Internet, YouTube, Google, Merriam-Webster's online dictionary, and more. The screens make it possible to reach people across the planet and put our thumbprints on the world.

So, yes, the screens are great. But we didn't always have them, and in some ways life was simpler. Without the screens, life was more about the face-to-face than Facebook; more about chitchat with friends and neighbors than tweets to the masses, and whatever came into your home was clearly invited because someone knocked and you opened the door.

When we look outward, we are more beautiful than
when we look inward.

Media is tricky—you just have to realize the screens have millions of doors. But your heart only has one, and you get to decide what comes into it and what goes out of it.

We cannot pretend the screens have no dangers. That would be idiotic. For one, they separate us from people and distract us from living fully in the moment, because when we are on our screen, our minds are in another place. So we have to understand screen etiquette. No screens while driving. No screens while in the grocery store line. No screens while a human being is sitting or standing across from you trying to talk to you. No screens at the table. And no screens during family time. It's not screen time all the time!

There is still value in reading a great book until the pages are worn from turning. Still value in handwritten letters and phone calls so your loved one can hear the tone of your voice. There is great value in board games and sports and handmade art and long walks with people you love.

The media can drive us to great destinations or horrible ones. For boys, it starts with video games. They play them for hours and hours and hours. Then, as they get older, a click of a button instantly funnels them into a world they have never seen—a world of pornography. This world, like the games, is endless. It leaves them feeling shamed, but now they know it's there.

It used to be the closest a boy could get to looking up a woman's skirt was running under the mannequins in the mall to take a peek. As he got older he might have rummaged through a *National Geographic* magazine or the underwear section in the JC Penney catalogue. When he grew up, he may have even ventured to the liquor store to peek at an X-rated magazine. But would he subscribe to it? Where would he have it sent? His house? His college dorm? No. So it wasn't that easily accessible.

Looking at pornography used to take thoughtful, premeditated effort and lots of hiding. Now it takes about this long: click, click, click, you're there. Mom's footsteps up the stairs, one click, gone.

After a hundred clicks, the boy's future wife won't be amazing anymore. After a thousand, he could be totally wrecked for her, tormented by the constant awareness of what is behind that screen—which isn't just in his room, but in his back pocket. The torture of what looks so desirable on the surface can derail him completely. He hasn't even met the tender wife of his youth yet or tasted her sweetness, and she's already sour.

For the girls, media images are ever so complicated. First off, you have the even mildly pornographic images to contend with—images you can't live up to, images which aren't even real. Even if the young woman glancing through Victoria's Secret knows her value is more than her body, her mind still becomes filled with images that present women as objects to be used, displayed, and sexualized, instead of holy beings made in the image of God. These airbrushed images of very young women posing as sex symbols have the potential to distort your image of yourself and the beauty of your body. Not good. *Not* of God.

Your generation of young women is forced to grapple with a generation of young men who have allowed the media to fill their heads with over-sexualized or pornographic images. Growing up, I didn't have nearly as many of those images to contend with: Hollywood actresses were generally classy and the sexy bombshells were few and far between. Now, almost all women in the media portray sex, even the Disney pop stars. It's a different world for you than it was for me, and it could be very hard on you should the one you love get captivated by the screen god. Both you and the one you date or marry must have strict boundaries around what you allow to come through your screen and into your heart.

The number of friends you have online or the
number of likes you get is no indicator of your value.

Some may say that what they see on the screen doesn't come into their hearts; it's just an image. But that's not true. Your eyes are the windows of your soul. Proverbs 4:23 tells us, "Above all else, guard your heart, for everything you do flows from it." There is only one place in the Bible where you will see those three words—*above all else*—and this is it. Above anything else you do, you are challenged, warned, and commanded to guard your heart, because it is the well of life for you. That means, guard it against jealousy. Guard it against comparison. Guard it against lust. Guard it against greed. Guard it against resentment. Guard it against idolatry. Guard it, guard it, guard it.

❀

All the focus on image in our world bears a burden for little girls. At one time or another, every little girl wants to be a star, for everyone to gaze at her image and *ooh* and *aah*. It used to be that only public personas had photos published of themselves. Now, anyone can be a star on the Internet. Social media sites give every girl the opportunity for people to gaze at her image and approve. She can post pictures of herself and everyone can give her instant admiration.

For lots of girls in search of approval—and especially for those who have suffered rejection—something twisted can happen. They can begin to think their likability is related to their online image. They can begin to place value on the number of likes or even ratings others put on their images. They can keep switching their profile picture in hopes of getting more attention, and when they get older they try sexy shots to earn approval. Now that little girl who ran around in princess crowns and gowns is posing like a Victoria's Secret model and everyone is rating her photos. "Aren't you gorgeous!" "You are so pretty!" "I want to get to know you!"

Women like taking pictures and making albums—it's natural for us. I did it when I was a kid, but we didn't have social media or digital photography, so the albums were just for me and my friends. The pictures stayed in my bedroom.

"My page *is* just for my friends," young women cry! I'm sorry, but no one has 358 friends. I have fifty, max. Twenty good friends. Ten who are super special. Five, max, who are so close I would share almost anything with them. And if I had a sleepover with those five, only two or three would actually sit with me and look at all the pictures in my album, and they would only do that because they really love me, not because they want to see every single one. The only person who wants to see every single picture of me is my mother.

I realize many young women are wise with how they craft their social media pages. But I also realize that far too many young women are obsessed with their own image. When I was a young model, I was obsessed with my own image too. I know how to make a diagnosis about this because I had the sickness!

What we see on the screen can be very deceptive. On the surface we see what looks like an online photo album or a fun way to share pictures or connect with friends. But beneath that veneer, trouble can be brewing. If a girl gets a text or is notified every time someone likes her picture or approves of her post, that's bad. Because every time you get a text, you are interrupted. You don't need to be constantly interrupted from your activities and time with loved ones to be told someone liked your picture or agreed with your thought. No wonder so many women are on a roller-coaster ride; no wonder they have image problems. Social media isn't just a way for people to connect; let's not be that naïve. It's also a way for kids to instantly and constantly approve and disapprove of one another.

Why are women and girls constantly changing their profile pictures? To keep up with the new look? Just to be girls and have fun? Or is it because some of them actually believe the lie of the masquerade—that their image as they present it in the media is the image they possess? Just as girls look to men, mirrors, magazines, and masks to reflect their beauty and value, so they look to the media for the same thing.

I mentored a girl who had this issue. She was my student in eighth grade, when I used to teach writing after I left the modeling industry. Rejected by her mother, dealing with her parents' divorce, feeling controlled and manipulated by her dad, she began cutting at age 12. She used to duck into my classroom at lunch because it was a safe harbor for her troubled heart.

Years later, she found me through Facebook. In communicating with her, I noticed her profile pictures were always changing to be more and more seductive. Never afraid to tell her the truth, I sent her a message, advising her to take the photos down, saying they dishonored her future husband and children. She soon called me to confess she had a full-fledged eating disorder, was promiscuous, stripping, addicted to drugs, delusional, and suicidal.

Together, she and I pounded on the door of Mercy Ministries, an excellent long-term treatment center for troubled young women.

When she graduated from Mercy, she called me to tell me how much God had illuminated things for her. Leaving a message on my phone, she said, "Call me back! I'm not well enough yet to have a cell phone—or Internet—or screens of any sort. So you can just reach me on the landline." At twenty-four years old, she was not well enough to have an iPhone. That tells you how poisonous looking at her own image was for her.

In our day, cameras pointed outward. They were used to capture memories. They were not mirrors. We couldn't take pictures of ourselves without them looking awkward and strained. Now, girls are pointing the camera at themselves, filling their phones with hundreds of photos of how they look. Yikes! We need to get back to reality here and test the images we are taking. A good filter is this understanding: Cameras are for capturing memories—and your best memories involve others, not just you.

Tell the screens to be still and turn your attention to your loved ones.

We might keep in mind that in schools, we take one school photo a year, and that image stands for how you look that year. One image is all you need. If you are changing your profile picture constantly, you probably need to focus on something other than yourself. When we look outward, we are more beautiful than when we look inward.

I need to make one final plea for your own well-being, and the future well-being of your husband and children. Remember that with digital media, when you post pictures of yourself via text, e-mail, or social sites, those pictures become public, and all someone has to do is click on a photo and save it to a hard drive. If the site doesn't allow them to do that, they can just take a picture of the screen and they have captured your image. Then, even if you regret publishing those photos of yourself and try taking them off the Internet, someone else has them saved. That person can text your photos or make a whole website of you without your knowledge.

The Internet is very deceptive. Anyone can pose as anyone. You are fooling yourself if you really think "only my friends can see my page." Any tech-savvy person can pose as a friend and get a window into your personal life if you post it online. It's not difficult at all. Any jerk can click on a girl's photo and pose as her. Then that jerk can say all kinds of horrible things about other people through "her" mouth. It's identity theft, but the Internet makes it easy, and it happens to girls in real life. Real lives are shattered by lies like these.

Worse, if you take sexual photos of yourself and share them, you have opened the door to turning your little dream into a nightmare. Whoever you sent that picture to can change his mind about you and decide he wants to let everyone know you are a slut. Or, he can show *one* person the picture—and that's enough to ruin your reputation. They can take that racy picture of you and put it on porn sites, and you can do nothing about it. Even sicker, someone can take a decent photo of a girl and Photoshop it to look like her head is on a nude body. Later in life, her husband and children will have to contend with those photos.

You get to decide what comes in through
the door of your heart.

You may think I'm being a little radical here, but believe me: It happens. I am warning you: Keep your privates private, keep your husband and kids sacred long before you have them, and just know you are getting a big thumbs-up from heaven and God's army of angels when you guard what is entrusted to you. Guard your heart, your body, your reputation, your relationships, your marriage, your kids, your future, and the possibility of your great influence in the world.

You are worth it.

Do You Like Me Now?

Some of the most beautiful women I know don't do social media—and if they do have a page, they don't broadcast their every good deed to the world. They teach kids to read in busy classrooms or sit face to face with troubled teens in counseling offices. They are the arms that hug the hurting and hand out tissues to dry tears without having to tell the world about it.

I am surrounded by people who don't need the thumbs-up from the world. My mother-in-law, Linda, has had a beautiful influence on my life and the life of this ministry, but she doesn't touch social media. My husband, who launched me into ministry, barely goes on Facebook but, through his heart for our sons, is raising two solid boys who will bless the world with their kind and gentle hearts. When Shane teaches them something great, he doesn't post it to see how many people will like or approve. He doesn't care if no one sees.

Caris, who founded the ministry with me, doesn't do social media. She goes mountain biking with girls. She takes them out on her boat and stays up late under the stars, hearing their stories and quietly, gently, ushering them toward a walk with God. God is the only one who sees and applauds her service; she posts no photos to the world to share her work in changing one life at a time. She simply doesn't need that kind of approval, and doesn't want the distractions of social media in her life.

I use Facebook and our ministry sends out messages through Twitter, Pinterest, and Instagram. But I have a purpose for it—to shine his light into the world. That's it. That's my only purpose, and I have to guard my heart from thinking people's *likes* are a reflection of me. And I have to shut down the screen when I get too into it and turn to the people I love.

Real intimacy, real friendship, real truth, and real life happen in the face-to-face and the heart-to-heart, something we can miss if we aren't careful. We need to remember that a friend isn't someone you just met or barely know; a friend is an intimately connected supporter of your life. And the number of friends you have online or the number of likes you get is no indicator of your value, nor does it measure your influence.

We also have to remember that privacy is good. At one time, who we were dating, who we liked, and the things we believed in stayed in our small circle. Now, many women make all of that public. It used to be that when a woman got asked to prom, it was a private moment between her and her date. Now it's blasted all over the screen—everyone gets a window into her world. Same goes for her engagement, wedding, babies, and so on.

And for some reason, many of us are under the impression that we need to tell everyone what we are doing and where we are all the time.

When does the personal publicity stop? When life gets hard? When dreams crash? When something bad happens? Or is that public too? For many it is. I have a friend who blasted her marital problems all over Facebook, and guess what? She got divorced, and everything she had written to her hundreds of "friends" about the situation became public record. Sad as it is, someday someone could print the whole saga out for her children. If they read everything she felt, said, and accused her husband of, it would only further devastate three kids whose hearts are already shattered.

I know another girl who blasted her friend drama all over the internet. Later, she wanted to resolve her problems with her friend. But guess what? That friend was too angry that their conflict was made public. They both lost a lifelong friend over it.

We have an issue with young women sharing things online that should be reserved only for their private diaries. Your "page" is not a diary. The Internet is the last place you share the personal trials of your life. Personal pain should be dealt with in the company of God, your closest friends (five, max), and wise counselors and mentors.

There is wisdom in following the example of Jesus's life. He spoke to the multitudes, sharing his teaching with as many as he could, and telling stories. Then he pulled aside his twelve disciples and shared the deeper meaning of the stories with them.

But his most intimate truth he shared only with those in his private circle. When he went up to the mountain he showed Peter, James, and John who he was. With Moses and Elijah present, Jesus showed his friends his glory, turning himself inside out. In that moment, he bared it all—not to the multitudes, but to his most intimate friends. And there, on that mountain, when he was as open and honest and real as he ever was going to get, God spoke to them. They heard his voice.

You know what Jesus told them when they came down from the mountain? *Keep this private. Don't tell anyone until I've been raised from the dead* (Matthew 17:9).

So, he spoke to hundreds of people sometimes. He shared the upclose journey of his life with twelve. And he bore it all with three, telling them to keep what they saw private.

Jesus believed in keeping some things secret, and he had the wisdom to know when a truth could free someone and when it could make them stumble. He didn't always want attention for every great thing he did. When he performed miracles, he didn't want it broadcast everywhere. In fact, he told people all the time: *Tell no one. Say nothing about this.*

That's right. He would do something great and tell people *not* to post it, *not* to share it, and of course they couldn't even *begin* to rate it.

Jesus's most beautiful interactions with people happened face to face, one on one. And when he suffered, he didn't look to the masses of people for answers; he looked to the Father.

As far as I can tell, he really lived for an audience of One.

Who's the Master?

It is the middle of the night. I have been writing a Bible study and my mind has been immersed in the Word for weeks. I've been studying the enemy and the differences between him and Christ. My brain is so wallpapered with what I've been reading that the Word is my only filter right now. I come outside of my office to make some tea and see that *The Bachelor* is on the screen. It's funny, it's crazy, it's completely ridiculous.

As I am waiting for my tea to boil, all of a sudden I see something true in a flash, like a film on fast-forward: *The Bachelor* is the lie of man. It's about worshipping man, believing what he thinks about you. *Extreme Makeover* is the lie of the mirror. It's about the poundage and the measurements declaring your worth. *Project Runway* is the lie of the magazine. It's the worship of outward beauty at the expense of others' worth. *Survivor* awards the best deceiver while *CSI* is all about murder.

Oh no! I think. The enemy is behind all of these TV shows! He is working his way into our home through the screen.

But here's the deal. I don't want to be rid of the screens. I love *American Idol*, and I'm not missing *Survivor* or *The Biggest Loser* next season. But it's not lost on me that "idol" is in the title and "loser" is a dig on overweight people. I'm not naïve enough to think the camera is going to record the pain of the girls who don't win *America's Next Top Model*; I know how many girls lose at the expense of the one who wins, and the one who wins may not win in the end. I understand that deceit is the basis of *Survivor*. I get that the screens glamorize sex before marriage.

It used to be *Leave It to Beaver* and *Happy Days*. Now it's *Modern Family* and *16 and Pregnant*. What about the video games? Boys used to play Pac-Man; now it's a bloodbath.

At some point we cross a line. It's no longer entertainment when the violence and overt sexuality are being replicated in our schools. Why are we so surprised when boys want to do target practice on real people and girls want to experiment with girls? In video games, boys get points for killing people; they get promoted. On TV, girls get attention for being a teen mom or making out with other girls. There are no repercussions on TV. In video games, there are no grieving mothers or outraged communities; death is a bonus. There is no human emotion involved. There is no loss of limb that ruins someone's dreams, no bullet that alters a person's working brain, no kids in physical therapy for the rest of their lives because of that bullet. And there certainly are no bars imprisoning the shooter for life. Instead, the shooter gets promoted.

We are fools to think the screen god doesn't have anything to do with the death of our values. Kids can go online and learn all kinds of evil things. The culture reflects what the screen instructs them to do. The influence is real and can make us sick, sick, sick.

Navigating the clash of the world and the Word is challenging but possible. You just have to keep your eye on the lighthouse, your ear tuned to the captain, and know how to steer clear of the dangers.

For every great battle, there is an enemy. He pursues you, trying to take you out of the race. Know your enemy. He exalts division. He exalts comparison. He exalts jealousy and envy. He exalts himself. He exalts deceit. He exalts the body. He exalts death. He exalts sexual sin. He exalts the outward appearance. He exalts everything but our great and awesome God.

And he works through the screen.

Let's throw a wrench into this discussion. What if God, not Satan, is the mastermind of the media? What if it was his idea in the first place to connect people across the globe through a screen? What if he wanted it first? What if he loves a great tragedy and a fantastic romance? What if he even has a vested interest in training our sons for combat? What if he wants them to know how to dodge a bullet and take out the enemy? What if he even wants them to win a battle when it looks like all odds are against them?

Hmm, sounds a lot like the God of the Bible.

Let's close this heavy-duty discussion with a funny story. During the first drafts of this book, I unplugged from all social media. Easy for me. But then toward the last few weeks of writing, I declared a fast from all screens except for this manuscript. I am so easily distracted that if I even open e-mail, I might not write all day. So on the final stretch, I refused e-mail. I insisted I would look at nothing on a screen but this book in your hands—which, to me, isn't a book. It's a dream and an assignment.

Real intimacy, real friendship, real truth, and real life happen in the face-to-face.

I really tried to fast from the screens, but I couldn't fully do it. Friends were texting me encouraging notes, and I felt like I had to respond—at least on the bathroom breaks! Next thing you know I'm passing notes with my friends via text, staring at another screen, committing adultery on my manuscript! Then I would get a text that said I had an important e-mail, so I would open the inbox to read it and see all the unimportant ones. Suddenly I'm unsubscribing from stuff, clicking all these buttons that really don't matter. And I couldn't keep up with the calendar without constant checking. I did my best—I really did—but it's almost impossible to completely get away from screens.

I was telling my hair stylist about my personal war with the screen, and she, who is never afraid to command her authority as a daughter of the King, turned to my cell phone and pointed her finger at it.

"Be still!" she commanded. "You! Be still!"

We do need to tell the screens to be still sometimes, and to turn our attention to our loved ones and see them only. We do need to stop wasting time on the screens and invest long hours in something that will last. And we do need to stop being mastered by the media and become masterful over it.

We can use the media as a vehicle to get us where we need to go. Or we can use it as a vehicle to pick up someone else who may be lost and get them where they need to go.

The possibilities are endless for how we can use media as a tool to shine a light into a lost and hurting world.

10 The Fifth Truth:

You Are a Chosen Ambassador

*"You are my witnesses," declares the LORD, "and
my servant whom I have chosen."*

ISAIAH 43:10

The Master Speaks

The media is communication for the masses. Sounds like a great way to reach people with my love. You can write books about my love, you can sing songs about my love, you can make videos and write poems and share thoughts about my love. Through the screen, you have the ability to spread the fragrance of my love farther and wider than any generation before you.

I want my people not only to speak to their neighbor, but also to speak to souls on the other side of the world.

Yet the Internet also opens up a window to the world, and the world's ways can openly funnel into your heart. Anything can be used for my glory or your shame; it's all in how you use it.

My people are working through the web to dig wells, feed the starving, and rescue my children from the abomination of human trafficking. People who understand their power over the web are using it as a vehicle to rescue the lost and help the suffering. Through the screen, my children inspire each other to believe in me and fight hard for the dreams I wove into their hearts.

Yet the ugly truth is that while one person uses a webcam to record a message of hope, another uses it to exalt evil. While one woman cries for the *rescue of the sexually abused, another places her own body up for sale. One woman shines a light of healing for girls with eating disorders while others create websites that twist a girl's image of herself. One woman pours out verses on social media while another pours out pain.*

In the world of the screen god anything goes, and that's not how things work with me. The screen god doesn't protect my children and never will. So it's up to you to guard your heart. You must know screens aren't safe unless you stay within the railings. You must wear a shield, wrap truth around you, wield your sword, and protect your mind. You must listen for my voice. I will tell you when it's time to get up on your feet, step away from the screen, and go face to face with the people who matter more.

Never believe the lie that your value is based on anything you see on a screen. Screens are distorting prisms; they can convolute and confuse your worth. Look up and away; look to me for your reflection.

Look through my eyes. Look through my eyes at everything you see.

God, Good

Have you ever noticed how the lead news stories are almost always bad news? Car crashes, escaped criminals, violence, disasters. By nature, the news is adversarial. Always looking for the shocker, the controversy, the tragedy, the accusation, the division, the deceit. It's not that we need to turn off the news, necessarily. We just need to realize that the news media capitalizes on the negative—and the media can lie to us.

Want God like you want life.

But God is not two-faced, and he is not a liar. He is a truth-teller and a straight-shooter. He is not a God of confusion, and he is not a God who profits from the bad news.

He is the God of the Good News.

The angel said to the shepherds, "Do not be afraid. I bring you *good news* that will cause *great joy* for all the people" (Luke 2:10). When Jesus stood up in the temple, he quoted Isaiah, saying, "God's Spirit is on me; he's chosen me to preach the Message of *good news* to the poor, sent me to announce pardon to prisoners and recovery of sight to the blind, to set the burdened and battered free, to announce, 'This is God's year to act!'" (Luke 4:18-19 MSG). God sent Jesus to bring "*messages of joy* instead of news of doom" (Isaiah 61:3 MSG). He is all about the good.

After Jesus ascended to heaven, the political climate of Paul's culture was in upheaval. The religious world was wracked with turmoil. Believers faced execution. What did the apostle tell them to do? Announce the bad news? Proclaim violence? Publish division and death?

No! He told them to preach the good news—to give messages of life and hope.

Lift up your eyes, he said. Fix them on the good. Meditate on what is "true, noble, reputable, authentic, compelling, gracious—the best, not the worst; the beautiful, not the ugly; things to praise, not things to curse" (Philippians 4:8 MSG).

Why does he tell us to focus on the life of Christ? To focus on the good? Because the more we focus on something the more we reflect it, and he wants us to "shine...like stars in the sky" as we hold out the word of life (Philippians 2:15). The world needs more goodness, more victory, more faith, more light, more healing, and more hope. The world does not need more pain and more trouble.

I wish the lead news stories were ones from ministries who are targeting the heart of darkness—the brothels of Greece and Southeast Asia and other parts of the world—where little girls are held captive. There are more slaves in the world today than at any point in human history: 27 million men, women, and children across the globe are forced into manual and sexual labor against their will. Ministries around the world are restoring whole communities with resources, education, medical care, safe houses, counseling, and job training. As one might rescue a child from a burning building, so heroes are rescuing women and girls from forced sex slavery.

That to me is good news; that is *headline* news. But mainstream media will not focus on it.

> Whatever you do, do it as one who represents
> her heavenly home.

I wish even my local news would feature my friend Polly's ministry, "We Are Cherished," where selfless women keep an open house with a hot dinner for women trying break free from the sex industry. The women at We Are Cherished are quietly going into the strip clubs on a regular basis and letting the dancers know they are made for more. If the dancers come to the Cherished House for dinner, women lovingly outfit them in beautiful clothes and help them get an education and start a new life in Christ. That's what I call beauty.

My former student who rose above cutting, suicidal thoughts, addiction, date rape, and bulimia, could be a great feature story. I can see it now: "A girl picks a better life! That's our lead story in tonight's news. And tonight at 11:00, two more girls set free in Cambodia! Freedom from strip clubs—good news from your own backyard!" Now that would be great. We could publish peace. We could proclaim salvation. We could focus on freedom.

❧

The media has multiple faces that are always changing, but God has one face: the face of the Most High. The face of God, Good.

There was a season in my life when I was so confused that I could not distinguish good from evil. I know that sounds crazy, but looking back on my life as a model and looking at the stormy season of my temple-clearing, I got seriously confused.

My counselor showed me this simple formula:

GOD = GOOD

DEVIL = EVIL

There is only one letter differing the spelling of *God* and *good* and one letter between *devil* and *evil*.

Our world calls evil good and good evil. But that couldn't be further from the truth. When something is good, it is God good. When something is evil, it is evil devil. It sounds simple, and it is. It helped me distinguish what was good in my life from what was not good; what was not healthy for me and what was. It also helped me develop boundaries around myself to protect my family from the evil devil.

I knew very little about healthy boundaries when I was a young woman. As daughters of God, we are to be vigilant about putting firm, solid boundaries around our hearts and bodies. Only good is allowed in. No evil. That means you have to be strong. You cannot let people or the latest trial control you. As my friend says, be a thermostat, not a thermometer. That means *you* set the gauge for the temperature; don't change your temperature with the latest trend or trial.

Be strong in your dealings with people; if they try to shoot arrows at you, put your hand up and say, "No more." If you have to walk away, do so. Do not set your foot in unholy places; remember you are holy. Don't wear a mask to hide your pain or make yourself look good; go unmasked with God and he will transform your pain into purpose. Be smart when it comes to the media. The moment something you see on the screen tries to steal, kill, and destroy, close the window. The moment someone compromises you, click "unfriend" and don't look back. If you need to delete to protect your heart, delete.

If we aren't wise, we can get swept away and forget what we are here for. We are not here to spend our lives in search of others' approval or allowing our need to be liked to suck away our precious time. We are here for a greater purpose, each one of us.

There are people in our own homes who need us to hold out our hands and hearts and show them they are more important than anything else. There are people in our own backyard who are trapped and afraid and hurt and abused, who need us to use our voices to speak words of life over them, and who may need a bed or a friend or a phone call or a meal. There are people all over the world who need us to reach out through the screen or through our lives to believe for miracles.

The world is in need of people who understand their purpose, their assignment, their calling, and their post.

Chosen

We cannot become overwhelmed by the rampant evil of our world and shut down, assuming we are powerless to do anything about it. We are not powerless. Those of us who are in Christ have the power that raised him from the dead living inside of us, and it's up to us to call on that power for victory.

When you mess up, remember: God loves messy girls. In fact, he's crazy about us.

Christ was called "The Chosen One." Then he turned around and said, "I have chosen you out of the world" (Luke 23:35; John 15:19). "You are my witnesses…and my servant whom I have chosen…I took you from the ends of the earth, from its farthest corners I called you. I said, 'You are my servant'; I have chosen you and not rejected you. So do not fear, for I am with you; do not be dismayed, for I am your God. I will strengthen you and help you; I will uphold you with my righteous right hand" (Isaiah 43:10; 41:9-10).

Jesus said, "In this world you will have trouble. But take heart! I have overcome the world" (John 16:33). I love how straightforward he is. *I chose you. I picked you. I believe in you and I will help you. I will never leave you and I will uphold you with my hand.*

As hard as things may get, we have to speak truth: *He who is in me has overcome the world. I am more than a conqueror. I am more than able to face the troubles of this life from a place of victory, because God already won.*

He picked us to represent him on this earth. He didn't pick us because we were great, but because we were weak, and in our weakness, he can be our strength. Paul calls us "Christ's ambassadors, as though God were making his appeal through us" (2 Corinthians 5:20). An ambassador is a diplomatic official of the highest rank, representing his home country in a foreign land. The ambassador reflects and enforces the beliefs and practices of the one who sent him.

You are an ambassador of the Most High God. But here's the good news: It's not about your power; it's about his. Only he can heal. Only he can free. Only he can restore and refresh and renew a soul. All we have to do is raise our hands and say, "Here I am, Lord! Send me!"

Where he sends us and how he sends us is up to him. Whether he sends us to Africa or to the local shelter; whether he sends us back home or abroad; wherever he sends us, we go knowing he is our guide. He is our good God and nothing he does will be outside of his faithful love for us.

No matter where we go as his daughters, lights, and ambassadors, on the inside, in the inner corridor of our hearts, let's go on our knees, raising hands high, pointing people not to ourselves, but to him.

Go and Tell One Girl

The Bible is full of great ambassadors. Paul, who had once stood by approving the execution of Christians, is a perfect example that our pasts do not dictate our futures. He lived as an opponent of the cross and then became its biggest proponent, writing over two-thirds of the New Testament. "To live is Christ and to die is gain," he wrote in Philippians 1:21.

I never set out to be an ambassador, or a light, or anything like that. I am simply a girl who was scooped up by the big hand of the Most High when I was hurting and lost. Since then, I've done a lot of things wrong. Time and again, I've landed on my knees. But I know this: No matter where you've been or what dark or broken roads you may have walked, or if the aisle of the church is worn with your footsteps, you are chosen to be his witness, his ambassador, his girl in a world that needs your light.

Whatever you do, do it as one who represents her heavenly home. And when you mess up, remember, God loves messy girls. In fact, he's crazy about us.

❀

The first Christ-following ambassador of the Good News, Mary Magdalene, was one messed-up chick. Jesus healed her of seven demons and then asked her to be the first to announce his resurrection.

Lift up your eyes. Fix them on the good.

Before she met Jesus, she was "possessed by demons," which in her day meant no one understood the source of her pain. "Demons" was a way for people to swipe their hand across her disease and say, "Well, the devil's got her by the throat."

I bet she felt tormented. Rejected. Unloved. Unworthy. Without Purpose. Lost. Aimless. Afraid. Misunderstood. Misshapen. Misnamed.

Then Jesus showed up on the scene—the one her soul longed for. He cast those demons out of her and healed her. What else could she do but follow his every step? She had no husband, no children. From Galilee, the very start of his ministry, she followed him and cared for his needs. I believe the pain of watching his crucifixion was the worst agony of her life; he was all she had. She had tasted love; she had feasted with her Redeemer, her Savior. But then they stole him away from her.

Sunday morning, when everyone was still home in bed, Mary came before dawn to the garden. She went inside the tomb, but he wasn't there.

"No!" she cried. "They have taken my Lord away and I don't know where they have put him!"

"Woman, why are you crying?" a voice asked her. "Who is it you are looking for?"

"Sir, if you have carried him away, tell me where you have put him, and I will go get him."

"Mary," the voice said, tender in her ears.

At first she thought he was the gardener, but then she realized it was Jesus! "Rabboni!" she cried. "Teacher!"

She tried to cling to him, but he backed up, warning her not to touch him, for he had not yet returned to the Father. I bet she wanted more than anything to hold on to him forever. I bet every muscle in her body said to stay. There she was, the new Eve, back in the Garden with God again. How horrible to have to leave!

But he had an assignment for her. He told her she must go to the disciples and tell them the good news: He had risen.

She had to let go. She had to turn from what she could see to what she could not see. She had to walk not by sight, but by faith. What she could see was only temporary; what she couldn't see was forever.

So she did what he told her to do. She ran.

In a strange way, I bet, "Mary, go" were the sweetest words she ever heard, because they meant he trusted her to hear his voice when he wasn't right there beside her in the flesh. They meant that he believed she, crazy Mary, could be a witness.

Of course the disciples didn't believe her, though. They had to go and see for themselves. But they discovered her words were true: Jesus had risen. He had conquered death. He had risen above all the suffering and all the pain. Then Jesus appeared to them again and gave them the same message he gave Mary: Go tell the good news.

Some legends say Mary went on to fast and pray in the wilderness, tormented by demons. Other legends say she went on to be a preacher on an island. I don't believe she disappeared into the wilderness endlessly. She had already been called out of the wilderness and given a purpose: She was a mouthpiece for the one her soul loved.

I'm sure the enemy tried to ruin her, tried to take her out, tried to destroy her witness and silence her, but I know he failed, because she still speaks to me today.

What do I hear when I hear Mary's voice? *Don't give up. You have been through a lot in your life, but your pain is not your mirror. Your suffering is not your end. In some ways, feeling it again transforms it into victory. People spat on Jesus, you know. They mocked him and whipped him and belittled him with the crown of thorns that pointed to his purpose.*

He doesn't just heal once. He heals in wishes and in waves. He loves you lavishly. He has called you with his voice. Follow it. Even when you don't know where it is leading, follow it. He will give you one word at a time; sometimes an open door, or closed one. If you are quiet and you listen, you will know your master's voice and it will never lead you wrong. Pray fervently. Love feverishly. Believe wildly.

Do not be afraid. Be strong and courageous. Fix your eyes on Jesus and he will light you up from the inside out. Go and tell!

❧

I once gave my testimony at a women's Christmas banquet. The women had erected a massive white tent and filled it with tables, candles, and endless lights. That evening the women filled the tent with a romantic excitement. Waiting behind a curtain to speak, I was on my knees. When I stood up, I was super energized and ready to get on the stage. I could feel my feet grow hot in my tall black boots, wanting to move up to the platform the moment I was called. I felt this fire in my soul and once the mic went on, it came out in my voice. That night, I could feel my Savior living inside of me as surely as I know he lives.

At the end of the talk, I asked if anyone wanted to accept him. As I offered the invitation, a dark, sweeping lull came over the room, like a hazy veil, and a sleepy stupor seemed to overcome the women. They all bowed their heads and kept them down.

"Who will believe?" I asked, the sound echoing in the massive tent.

Then, on the far side of the room, out of five hundred women, I saw one girl. She raised her hand high, reaching toward the ceiling. Then her whole body rose out of her seat, and she stretched her hand high and tall as she could, overextending it. She was the only one to receive Christ that night.

From the stage, I saw a picture of the world—heads down, hearts closed, darkness like a veil blanketing souls. The enemy wanting everyone to stay down, to stay asleep. And then I saw the faith of one girl.

Are you her? That one girl who will stand up in the crowd and say, "I believe"?

I was that girl once, in a world where the storm cloud hung low and it felt like nobody could see. I wanted God like I wanted life, and I found the one my soul loved.

Your identity is more powerful than your brokenness.

Something happens when God gets ahold of one girl: He gets ahold of another girl, and another girl, and another. The next thing you know, we are shaking the earth with our faith, stomping our boots like Mary, freeing the captives with swords in our hands, shining lights like moonlit cities, washing feet with the love of our Savior, changing the world one life at a time.

After God gets ahold of one girl, the girl is never the same, and neither is the world around her.

Redeemed

My cheek is still pressed to the couch and I wouldn't open my eyes if I could. No way—I am still in my vision of the temple, and Jesus just winked at me from the center. I can see all the people praising him in unison. It feels like the fullness of joy.

Then suddenly the slideshow changes. Now I am back at the meadow where I started, inside a large wooden bunkhouse. There are lots and lots of bunks, and all my girlfriends are there. We are all hugging our pillows and snuggled up in our blankets, eagerly anticipating a bedtime story.

Larger than life, Jesus is sitting on the edge of a bunk. He is holding a huge book. The Book of Stories is written on the spine.

"Would you like me to tell you a story?" he asks.

"Yes, Lord! Oh, yes!" we say, our voices in harmony.

Then he opens the giant book and reads us a story.

Next to how much I love him, I love the temple. And next to how much I love the temple, I love a sleepover. And next to how much I love a sleepover, I love a great story.

The slideshow changes.

It is morning. I am wrapped in a woolen blanket, sitting in a rocker on the deck of the bunkhouse, overlooking the meadow. Jesus brings me a piping hot cup of fresh coffee and sits down beside me.

The meadow is before us, an endless field of wheat-colored grass and wispy flowers. Beyond it is the thicket of woods, and beyond that, the hills and mountains in the distance. I turn to smile, and there, right beside him, is my beloved Shane. Coffee in his hand, sitting in the rocker on the other side of Jesus.

Shane and Jesus start laughing and being silly together. As personal as the temple was for me, Jesus is equally as personal with Shane.

The slideshow changes, and our whole family is walking through the meadow. The children are draped all over Shane's robust and redeemed frame. Behind them I follow, walking in peace and joy.

Circling our heels are our precious dogs, running and bounding in the field.

Everything is redeemed. And it is more beautiful than you know.

***

There was a time in my life when I felt like someone had swept my feet out from underneath me and I was broken in little pieces all over the ground. I felt like I should stop speaking, stop writing, and just be silent. I felt like I should close up shop and be done. I decided I was too messy, too broken, too confused to get this ambassador thing right.

Then we went to church one day. The huge crowd of people were singing and praising and I was just crying. Glad when we could sit down, I sunk into the chair, my shoulders slumped forward.

Our ministry had just produced some special bracelets with the identity message on them. They had five symbols to remind you that you are God's daughter, creation, temple, light, and ambassador.

I was wearing the bracelet for the first time that day. Feeling horrible, I was looking down at it, fiddling with the little charms.

I'm not a princess! I thought. *I'm not a temple! I'm no ambassador. I have no light. I'm not any of these things. I'm not!*

I didn't hear a word of what the pastor said. But then I looked up. "Point One," he recited. These words came across the screen, one letter at a time:

YOUR IDENTITY IS MORE POWERFUL THAN YOUR BROKENNESS.

My sister, my friend, your identity is more powerful than your brokenness.

Don't ever stop believing. Don't ever stop loving. Don't ever stop living out the identity that God assigns you. Your name is Daughter, Creation, Temple, Light, Ambassador.

You are an overcomer. You are more than a conqueror. By the word of your testimony and the blood of the Lamb, you shall overcome.

Your one true mirror is God, and he reflects who you really are. He who is in you is greater than he who is in the world. Don't give up. Fight the good fight. Finish the race.

You are more than what men think. You are more than what you see in the mirror or what the magazines say. You are more than the mask you wear and more than the many faces of the media.

You are his Beloved Daughter.

You are his Precious Creation.

You are his Beautiful Temple.

You are his Shining Light.

You are his Chosen Ambassador.

And you are a World-Changer, changing the world one heart at a time.

P.S. Pass It On

My heart for this message is that you would pass it on. If you felt impacted by this book in any way, share your thoughts. Post it, share it, Tweet it, write a review, write me a letter, or hand the book to a girl in school when you are done with it. Share the lies and the truths with a younger girl coming up the road behind you or an older woman still in the race. Lead a small group using the devotions at the end of the book. Share them with your sister, aunt, best friend, or mom. Just do me a favor and pass the baton. Too many women and girls focus on the ways we are different instead of the ways we are the same.

To be a world-changer, your voice must rise high and strong above the lies of the culture. Teach others the beautiful truth of who they are in God's eyes.

To him, we are all Daughters, Creations, Temples, Lights, Ambassadors.

Pass it on.

The Beautiful Truth

30 Days of Devotions

I welcome you to use these devotions as quiet moments alone with God or in group discussion. They will help you dispel the lies the world tells about your value and deepen your understanding of the identity you have in Christ. Each day has a "jewel for your journey," a special message from the Word of God. Hold these jewels close to your heart. They will help you navigate your life's journey with power and purpose.

Day 1

A Man or a Mirror?

Jewel for Your Journey

LORD, what are human beings that you care for them, mere mortals that you think of them? They are like a breath; their days are like a fleeting shadow.

PSALM 144:3-4

When we turn away from the "mirror of man" and turn instead into the "mirror of the Word," we learn some interesting things about people. Genesis 1:27 tells us that when God created human beings, he made man and woman "in his own image." People are the only created beings made in the likeness of God. We reflect God and are given supremacy over all other created beings.

But people are *not* gods. You are not made in the image of man, so you must be careful to not let people define you. People don't decide your worth; God does.

Even though we are made in the image of God, people can die in an instant. Our jewel for today's journey says people are "like a breath," our days are a "fleeting shadow." James 4:14 says, "you are a mist that appears for a little while and then vanishes." Isaiah 40:6-7 says, "All people are like grass…The grass withers and the flowers fall, because the breath of the LORD blows on them."

What does that mean for us? Man is a breath, a shadow, a mist, grass? It means that people, as wonderful or as evil as they might be, are only human. They are here one day and gone the next. Life is short.

We can love people, appreciate people, honor people, forgive, serve, and care for people, but we cannot base our identity, value, or happiness on what people think about us. If we do, we are surely in for a roller-coaster ride!

Remember, people are made in the image of God and deserve total respect and honor. But only God shows you your perfect reflection, and in the mirror of his face, every day, all day, you are loved, precious, beautiful, and valuable to him, no matter what people do or don't do for you, no matter what people do or don't say about you. Don't hang your hat on people. Hang it on God!

> *These people are nothing but grass, their love fragile as wildflowers. The grass withers, the wildflowers fade, if God so much as puffs on them... True, the grass withers and the wildflowers fade, but our God's Word stands firm and forever.*
>
> ISAIAH 40:6-8 MSG

Day 2

God Is Not a Man

Jewel for Your Journey

God is not a man, so he does not lie. He is not
human, so he does not change his mind.

NUMBERS 23:19 NLT

People change their minds all the time. A guy may declare his love and dedication to you and then change his mind. Not fun, and can be very hurtful. But you too change your mind. You may believe someone is your best friend for life but then change your mind about her. You may change your mind about a career path or place to go to college. This is a normal part of becoming who you are. But when people change their minds about us in relationships, it can feel crushing.

In the modeling industry, people would say I was what they wanted one day, but a few weeks later, they'd decide they preferred someone else. That may have been for a magazine ad, but it still had an effect on my heart. I could never be "good enough" for people all the time. They were always changing their minds about me.

The beautiful thing about God is that he says it straight. He says in our jewel for today's journey, "I am not a man!" "I do not lie!" "I do *not* change my mind." It's great to have someone in your life who will never lie to you, never change his mind about you. In fact, Hebrews 6:18 says it is *impossible* for God to lie. Can you imagine having a relationship with someone who *can't* lie to you? Someone who is only capable of telling you the truth? That's having a relationship with God. His Word is truth, and every day, it's up to you whether you are going to let people define you or God define you.

God won't ever leave you or turn his back on you. In life, there may be some people who turn their backs on you. That happens to everyone. Most of us deal with heartbreak and disappointment, and we *all* deal with death. People, as much as we love them, have the freedom to leave us or change their minds about us, and they will definitely die at some point!

But God doesn't die, doesn't leave us, can't lie to us, and won't ever turn his back on us. Now that's a solid foundation to stand on. So no matter how man has changed his mind about you, remember that you are loved by God. You can hold your head high because God is on your side—forever!

> *I the* Lord *do not change.*
> Malachi 3:6

Day 3

Prince Charming or Prince Perfect?

Jewel for Your Journey
All fall short of the glory of God.
ROMANS 3:23

It is so easy to get confused with the *prince* thing. The fairy tales suggest the prince is perfect. He is not only charming, but he is the savior of our lives. He defeats the enemy; he rescues us; he restores our fortunes and dreams. And while God may move through a man to help and even heal us, God never says that the man is our salvation, or that we should make princes our refuge.

Every human being falls short of perfect. But not God! Psalm 18:30 says, "As for God, his way is perfect." James warns us that no man can always say or do the right thing. He writes, "We all stumble in many ways...No human being can tame the tongue" (James 3:2,8). In other words, while the word of the Lord is flawless, the words of man can be flawed. Sometimes they can even be destructive and hurtful. This is why we cannot hang on every word people say about us, whether good or bad.

God never sins in his words to us. He never falls and never makes mistakes. But every man stumbles, sins, falls, and some fall hard.

Don't be deceived by the fairy tales. A true prince is a man who protects, shields, honors, encourages, and inspires you to be the best you can be. But every prince needs a king—and that king is Jesus.

Wait for a son of the king. Save your sexuality for him because you are precious and so is he. Preserve your purity and beauty for the one true prince God has destined for you. But remember, while the prince may be charming, he'll never be perfect.

Look into the face of the Perfect One for your beauty, value, and security. The more I do this, the more joyful I am, because I am secure in who I am in God's eyes! Don't expect people to be God for you. That job is taken by the only one who will ever be perfect—Jesus.

> *As for God, his way is perfect: The LORD's word is flawless; he shields all who take refuge in him.*
>
> 2 SAMUEL 22:31

Day 4

A Prince or a Castle?

Jewel for Your Journey

It is better to take refuge in the LORD than to trust in humans.
It is better to take refuge in the LORD than to trust in princes.

PSALM 118:8-9

God is so serious about us not making "people" or even "princes" our refuge that he warns us powerfully in Jeremiah:

> Cursed is the one who trusts in man...That person will be like a bush in the wastelands; they will not see prosperity when it comes. They will dwell in the parched places of the desert, in a salt land where no one lives.

> But blessed is the one who trusts in the LORD, whose confidence is in him. They will be like a tree planted by the water that sends out its roots by the stream. It does not fear when heat comes; its leaves are always green (Jeremiah 17:5-8).

What a drastic difference between one who trusts in man and one who trusts in God! The one who puts his faith in humans is "cursed" like a dry bush in a deserted desert. But the one who puts his faith in God is like a healthy tree planted in a deep riverbed; even in a year of drought, that person flourishes. In Psalm 144:2, David calls God his "refuge." A refuge is a protection, a safe harbor, a retreat or strong fortress—like a castle! He says we can run to God and be safe.

Do you get your confidence from people liking you? Approving of you? Applauding you? Or do you get your confidence from the Lord, who loves you no matter what? It's easier to put our confidence in something we can see than to put it in God, who we can't see. But we absolutely have to learn to get our confidence from him because only he is our Rock of Refuge. Only he holds a mirror for us that never changes.

God's Word warns us about something the fairy tales don't: Princes are not castles. Only God is a castle that is never shaken, a fortress through every season of life. Those who put their hope in people will find themselves empty and dry, but those who put their hope in God will flourish like a healthy tree. Who will you make your refuge today?

> *He is my loving God and my fortress, my stronghold and my deliverer, my shield, in whom I take refuge.*
>
> PSALM 144:2

A Buried Treasure

Jewel for Your Journey

The kingdom of heaven is like a merchant looking for fine pearls. When he found one of great value, he went away and sold everything he had and bought it.

MATTHEW 13:45

Did you know God sold everything he had to buy you? It's true! When I think of everything I have, I might consider my house or car or clothes at first, but if someone asked me what I have of great value, I would say my husband and children. When it comes down to it, the only things of great value we really have are the people we love. God had *one* son, and he so loved you that he gave that son up in exchange for *you*.

The crazy thing is the world didn't recognize Jesus as God's Son. When he called God *Father*, people called Jesus a liar. And when Jesus proved he was God's Son by miraculously healing a lame man, raising a little girl from the dead, and feeding thousands with a few broken loaves of bread, everyone did not bow down and call him "King." Instead, they grew into a mad mob demanding his death by crucifixion. They crowned him with a spiky crown of thorns and whipped him till his body was bloody, broken, and marred. They nailed him with huge spikes to a heavy wooden cross. They hurled insults at him and spat on him, making fun of him and laughing. Can you imagine how horrible that must have been?

People literally bullied Jesus to death.

But what one man calls trash, God calls a pearl. Jesus has such great value that anyone who believes he is the son of God who died for their sins and rose again has eternal life with the Father. He is so valuable that believing in him gives us a heavenly home that lasts forever. When you get there, you will walk with him and talk with him in the cool of the day, as Eve once did! You will be in a perfect, renewed earth and there will be no tears.

Jesus said, "I am the resurrection and the life. The one who believes in me will live, even though they die; and whoever lives by believing in me will never die. Do you believe this?" (John 11:25-26).

If your answer is yes, then Romans 10:9 declares: "If you declare with your mouth, 'Jesus is Lord,' and believe in your heart that God raised him from the dead, you will be saved."

It's that simple. You can accept Christ as your Lord right where you are—and you can help a friend do it right where she is too!

Our jewel for today's journey says the kingdom of heaven is like a merchant looking for fine pearls, and when he finds one of great value, he sells everything he has to buy it.

The pearl he is talking about is you. You are a fine pearl of great value, and your heavenly Father loves you so much he gave everything he had to buy you.

How will you respond to that today? How will that truth change you?

> *For God so loved the world that he gave his one and only Son, that whoever believes in him shall not perish but have eternal life.*
>
> JOHN 3:16

Day 6

Live! Be Mine!

Jewel for Your Journey

I put…a beautiful crown on your head.

EZEKIEL 16:12

My heart aches for hurting people. I hate that there are children in the world who don't have Moms and Dads that love and care for them. I hate that children are abused and left alone.

Maybe I feel this way because as a young woman, I had moments of abuse and moments of abandonment in my life as a model. I tasted emotional pain, took in cruel words, and felt the sting of rejection. At one time, I felt so alone that I wanted to die.

But then God passed by. I met a girl who shared Christ with me. I met people handing out Bibles in a park. I encountered church. I dove into the Word, and I felt God say to me, "Live! Be mine!" I realized that I didn't have to live my whole life wallowing in what people thought about me or how they criticized or praised me. I could find my worth in God. I could decide that how God saw me was more important than how others saw me. I could decide it was okay to not be perfect. I could be flawed, and at the same time, free.

But for a long time, I carried the mess of my past with me. I carried the hurt. Into my adulthood, I was deeply angry with those who disappointed and discarded me. Even though most people couldn't see it on the surface, at the bottom of heart dwelled the shadows of shame. The chains of anger and blame were dousing my light.

Then a new day came when God passed by again and told me it was high time to wash away all that yucky grime from my past. He washed off my shame by helping me forgive myself of my worst mistakes. And he washed off the hurt by helping me forgive those who had hurt me. Instead of wearing my anger like a cloak that weighed me down, I began to wear a new lighter gown—of joy.

Unforgiveness is a joy-stealer. When we don't forgive others, we carry the heavy burden of their sins on our own backs, and it's tough to stand tall and radiant with a heavy load on your back. Your heavenly Father knows how you've been hurt, and he asks that you hand that load of hurt over to him so he can carry it for you. He's much stronger than you are anyway, and he can handle the weight of your pain.

So today, before you sleep, forgive. Let go. Remember, as you let go, that God lets go of your sins too, and you become free to stand tall, wearing the crown of the Daughter of the King, radiant because of what he did for you.

> *Forgive, and you will be forgiven.*
> LUKE 6:37

Day 7

Secure in Love

Jewel for Your Journey

*Let the beloved of the LORD rest secure in him, for
he shields him all day long, and the one the
Lord loves rests between his shoulders.*

DEUTERONOMY 33:12

In his writing, the apostle John referred to himself as "the beloved of
the Lord" or "the one the Lord loved." Was he overly confident or
was he on to something?

John identified so much with the love Jesus had for him that it
became his identity. In his walk with Jesus, he wasn't just "John." His
encounter with Christ gave him a new name. He became "the one the
Lord loved," the "Beloved of the Lord."

In your hardest moments, or even in your day-to-day life, can you
imagine yourself crawling into your heavenly Daddy's lap and resting
your head on his heart, relaxing your whole body between his massive
strong shoulders? In that place, you are secure. You are safe. He guards
you all day long.

What thing in your life feels out of control? What scares you? What
are you afraid of? What do you desperately need? Your heavenly Daddy
beckons you to come and crawl into his lap. You can cry there, you can
ask for what you want, and you can be real because you are totally and
completely accepted by him.

The poet David said, "He is my fortress, I will never be shaken"
(Psalm 62:2).

Allow him to be your fortress, your resting place, your shield. Princess, you are safe in your Father's arms. You are the Beloved of the Lord, the "one the Lord loves."

> *Whoever fears the* LORD *has a secure fortress.*
>
> PROVERBS 14:26

Day 8

Hold on to Your Crown

Jewel for Your Journey

*Hold on to what you have, so that no
one will take your crown.*

REVELATION 3:11

It wouldn't be right for me to tell you that you wear a beautiful crown without warning you that someone will try to steal it from you. Jesus called the devil both a liar and a thief. Satan will lie to you, trying to tell you that you are never enough the way you are. He will try to steal your identity as God's daughter. Remember, every Disney princess had an enemy who was after her heart. I need to be clear with you up front: There is an enemy bent on destroying you.

If the enemy can divide your heart, he will. If he can fill you with shame and fear, he will. If he can separate you from God and family, he will. His entire goal is to destroy you, thus devouring your light and the potential of your good influence in the world.

Princess, the enemy is after your crown. He wants to knock it off. He wants to discredit you. He is going to try to lead you into sin. He is going to try to get you to question God's and your parents' boundaries and convince you that you don't need them. He is going to make sin look delicious to you, knowing it separates you from your Father. If he can devour your place in the kingdom, he will do it.

So what are you to do? You can use your authority as the daughter of the King to command the enemy to leave you alone. Use the Word of God against him. Every time the devil tempted Jesus, Jesus responded with Scripture. Why? Because it is the sword of the Spirit and it will slay the enemy at your feet.

Make a decision now to hold on to your crown. To wear it well, and to never, ever let anyone steal it from you. Your identity as a daughter of God is the only identity that is eternal. It gives you value, beauty, and worth that will stand the test of time.

Big girls fight with swords. We are not afraid of the devil and his schemes. We practice wielding our swords by studying the Word of God. No matter what we face, we rise again, wearing indestructible crowns and fighting with weapons of spiritual warfare. Together we fight in the name of the King, and together, we will win!

> *The thief comes only to steal and kill and destroy; I have come that they may have life, and have it to the full.*
>
> JOHN 10:10

The Magic Mirror

Jewel for Your Journey

We are...created in Christ Jesus to do good works,
which God prepared in advance for us to do.

EPHESIANS 2:10

In *Snow White and the Seven Dwarfs,* the evil queen is mesmerized with the mirror.

"Slave in the magic mirror, come from the farthest space!" she cries, the black wings of her cape arching behind her. "Through wind and darkness I summon thee: Speak!" The mirror fills with flames. "Let me see thy face!" she howls.

Through shadowy spirits, a mask emerges. "What wouldst thou know, my queen?"

"Magic mirror on the wall, who is the fairest one of all?"

"Famed is thy beauty, majesty," the mask says. "But hold, a lovely maid I see. Rags cannot hide her gentle grace. Alas, she is more fair than thee...Lips red as a rose. Hair black as ebony. Skin white as snow."

"Snow White?" the queen rages, her ghoulish eyes swelling with fury.

The evil stepmother is so obsessed with her appearance that she cannot appreciate the youthful beauty of her own daughter.

We should pay attention to the way the mask in *Snow White* emerges from fire—just as the devil dwells in the fiery furnace. Remember, princess, there is always an enemy lurking to steal your destiny. If he can work through the mirror he will. He will try to get you to focus so much on your appearance that you, like the queen, play the comparison game with other girls. *Who is the prettiest?* you will ask, jealous of others' beauty. The devil wants to grip you in jealousy, because when you are jealous, you are not powerful. You cannot celebrate the gifts in others and grow your own gifts. If he can catch you in the claws of jealousy, he can silence you. Our jewel for today's journey says you were created to *do* good, not just *look* good.

You were made to beautify the world with who you are. There are special things about you that make you unique. Find out what those things are. Grow your gifts. Don't waste your time and energy being jealous of others. Find out what you are good at and don't ever be afraid to applaud others.

Your beauty is not found in the magic mirror. Your beauty is found in who you are on the inside and the imprints you make on the earth.

Fan into flame the gift of God, which is in you.

2 Timothy 1:6

Day 10

Our Battle

Jewel for Your Journey

Our struggle is not against flesh and blood.

EPHESIANS 6:12

If you ever battle your weight or skin or health, remember your battle is not really with your body. Your battle is with the enemy.

As women, we can get focused on what we perceive as our "flaws." My breasts are small; my skin is breaking out; my hair is untamable. Others battle disease or obesity. Others still are obsessed with having the ideal body, which they will never have. But our war is not with flesh. Our war is with the enemy, who tries to get us to battle our own bodies instead of care for them.

We are taught by our culture to control our bodies, but we are never fully in control and never will be. We rest in our bodies by surrending control. When we do this, we get our focus off ourselves, off others, and on God.

When we demand perfection from our bodies, we put our spirits in prison. When we grant our bodies the grace to be flawed, treating them with tender loving care, we are free in our spirits to be beautiful from the inside out, no matter what state our bodies are in.

Even when Jesus's body was broken on the cross, his battle wasn't against the people beating him; it was against the devil. Even in his death, Jesus won because he surrendered his body to the Father. Entrust your body to him; it is a spiritual act of worship that is beautiful to the One who made you.

I urge you, brothers and sisters, in view of God's mercy, to offer your bodies as a living sacrifice, holy and pleasing to God—this is your true and proper worship.

ROMANS 12:1

Day 11

Renewed Day by Day

Jewel for Your Journey

*Outwardly we are wasting away, yet inwardly
we are being renewed day by day.*

2 Corinthians 4:16

There are a few things we must understand about our bodies. First, they are the packaging for our spirits, so they are important. The Bible says your body is "holy." That means the way you care for your body and the way you see it matters.

When we look in the mirror, we all want to be the best we can be that day. That means we exercise, eat healthy, and care for our skin, hair, and nails. We can wear light makeup that highlights our features. We can dress our bodies well in clothing that complements our figures—not too tight or skimpy, and not sloppy either. We honor our bodies as daughters of the King.

We don't let our bodies go to waste by ignoring them. When we eat junk, use drugs, or overeat, we aren't honoring the fact that our bodies are houses for God's Spirit.

Each of us is made in God's image. The world offers plenty of healthy food and ways to stay fit. We can choose to honor our bodies as the packages for our spirits and present ourselves beautifully, as long as we understand that real beauty comes from the spirit of love within us.

But we must know the reflection in the mirror is not a reflection of our value—good or bad. Consider a woman with a curvy figure and long, flowing red hair. Suddenly, she gets cancer. When she loses her hair and her figure, she doesn't lose her beauty. Her will to fight for life and the determination to live big as long as she lives—these are the qualities that make her gorgeous.

When Christ comes again, or bodies will be transformed in a flash; we will be given new, spiritual bodies (1 Corinthians 15:44,51-53). As long as we are on earth, our bodies will waste away outwardly. But inwardly we can be renewed day by day. This is the activity of the Spirit of God inside us. He refreshes and renews us, changing us to become more like him, so that his Spirit within us glows brighter and more beautiful all the time.

> *And so we are transfigured much like the Messiah, our*
> *lives gradually becoming brighter and more beautiful*
> *as God enters our lives and we become like him.*
>
> 2 CORINTHIANS 3:18 MSG

Day 12

A Poor Reflection

Jewel for Your Journey

Now we see things imperfectly, like puzzling reflections in a mirror, but then we will see everything with perfect clarity. All that I know now is partial and incomplete, but then I will know everything completely, just as God now knows me completely.

1 CORINTHIANS 13:12 NLT

When we look in the mirror, what we see looks like a perfect reflection. It looks crystal clear. But your reflection in the mirror is only a part of who you are. Our jewel today says that only when we see Jesus face to face will we see clearly. Life on earth is a shadow of the things to come. When Jesus brings us to our heavenly home, everything will be perfect. There will be no pain, no disease, no tears, no broken bodies, no broken hearts.

One day, you will walk with God and talk with God in his renewed creation. There will be no striving for things to be different. No accidents. No death. No sickness. Just joy. The fullness of heaven's expanse; perfect fulfillment at every turn.

What's cool about this is that even though we see only "a part," God knows all. He wove us together in the depths of the earth; he sees when we rise and when we fall; he formed our inmost beings (Psalm 139:13-16). Everything about you, God knows.

You are fully known. Fully seen. Fully loved. And someday, you will see him fully too. So do not fix your eyes on what you see day to day; fix your eyes on him—the perfect one who will come back for you and wash away all the imperfections (2 Corinthians 4:18).

So we fix our eyes not on what is seen, but on what is unseen, since what is seen is temporary, but what is unseen is eternal.

2 CORINTHIANS 4:18

Day 13

The Artist

Jewel for Your Journey

God saw all that he had made, and it was very good.

GENESIS 1:31

God is a giver. The first thing he did was give us light. He created the night. He formed sky. He spoke dry ground into existence and called it land. He created plants and fruit-bearing trees, and lit the sky with the sun, moon, and stars. He filled the water with living creatures, the sky with birds to fly, and the land with animals. Finally, he made man in his image, in his own likeness, to rule the earth and the creatures in it. He blessed the first couple and gave them everything they needed to flourish.

Just as he made the land, sky, sea, and stars, he made you. Psalm 139:13 says his eyes saw your unformed body when he wove you together in your mother's womb. He ordained your days before you took your first breath.

Yet according to studies, only two percent of women believe they are beautiful. Why? Because they do not get their image of themselves from their Creator. They get their image from the media. They compare themselves to women in the media and think they are not beautiful.

But when you take in all that God created, and realize that *you* are "the work of his hand," marvelously made, you can change that statistic. You can be the one who knows who she is—the handiwork of the Master Artist.

You are God's workmanship, craftsmanship, and poetry. If you've ever crafted a poem, knit a blanket, or molded a vase, you know the act of creating is an act of love. When God created you, he had vision for you. No detailed, painstaking effort was too much work to bear. He gave all his heart and soul into the making of you.

So what will be the poem of your life that he writes through you? What will the canvas of your days look like?

I praise you because I am fearfully and wonderfully made; your works are wonderful, I know that full well.

PSALM 139:14

Food

Jewel for Your Journey
I have food to eat that you know nothing about.
JOHN 4:32

Eating disorders are complicated. There are physical, mental, emotional, and spiritual forces in conflict. They require empathetic and strategic care. Yet the idealistic part of me just wants to have an awesome dinner party for girls with eating disorders. I'd invite Jesus, we'd have a banquet, and they'd see that "life is more than food, and the body more than clothes" (Luke 12:23). They'd see God *gave* us food to enjoy. They'd see that when people gather at a table to break bread and invite him, the presence of Jesus joins them.

They'd see that Jesus is the bread of life, the manna from heaven, and only he satisfies their soul hunger.

I have a friend who thinks in heaven we will only eat the bread and wine of communion. He is a serious Bible scholar but I beg to differ. I believe in heaven there will be pasta. Olives. Fruit. Veggie dip. Bakeries. Coffee. Ice cream. And definitely peanut butter and chocolate. It's going to be a party and we are going to enjoy the richest of the earth's fruits. And in the presence of God, our souls' cravings will be completely satisfied.

Ask Jesus, *What is your will for me? What is your work for me?* The answers to these questions are food for your soul, food that cannot be bought. Food that satisfies your soul hunger. To do the will of the one who sent us…this is the bread of heaven. Mysterious, satisfying manna. Let's eat!

> *Life is more than food, and the body more than clothes.*
>
> LUKE 12:23

Day 15

A Fortress Around Your Heart

Jewel for Your Journey

Above all else, guard your heart, for
everything you do flows from it.

Proverbs 4:23

To guard your heart is to treat it as priceless, to believe it is a jewel worth preserving. This verse doesn't suggest we take a casual watch over our hearts like we would a few dollars. It implies a diligent, watchful, careful awareness in how we guard them.

There are many ways to guard your heart—through what you see, hear, say, and expose yourself to. It's not the popular thing to do. The popular thing is to watch R movies before you are old enough, to dress seductively, to date early, and to have sex when you "feel" like you are ready.

If you ever visit the Vatican in Rome, you will see imposing guards standing out front. These men wear feathered hats and carry spears, but I bet they are packing weapons beneath their costumes. The guards represent security for the Vatican. They are there to make sure no one threatening the welfare of the sacred church enters in.

In your life, you are the guard over your heart. If you gaze too long at images that make you feel less than enough; if you expose your mind or body to sexual sin; if you ingest drugs or drink in excess; if you allow jealousy, hatred, or bitterness to take root in your heart, you aren't being a very good guard.

Don't expect anyone else to guard your heart for you. That's your job. Why? Because everything you do in life will flow from your heart. Your relationships, friendships, work—everything is an outpouring of your heart. Seems like it is worth protecting. How can you be a vigilant guard over your heart? What do you need to take care to protect yourself from? What will you allow inside the gates of your heart and what will you not allow in?

Maybe you can make a list of things—like respect, love, and kindness—that you will allow inside the gates of your heart. And make a list of things that you will not allow inside—things like disrespect, cruelty, and dishonesty. Remember, you are the guard, and it's up to you to protect the treasure that you are.

A heart at peace gives life to the body.
PROVERBS 14:30

Day 16

Test the Spirits

Jewel for Your Journey

Dear friends, do not believe every spirit, but test the spirits to see whether they are from God.

1 John 4:1

Fashion images have a way of making everything look good. Whether you are perusing your favorite social media site or flipping through a magazine, you see an average of 700 media images a day. That's a lot of input. Images have a way of wallpapering our minds. They can subtly form our definitions of beauty and worth.

But I'll remind you again: Just because something looks good doesn't mean it *is* good. Fashion magazines portray premarital sex as normal and healthy. The more we take in the world's viewpoint, the more acceptable sin becomes. Check out what the Bible says about this: "Woe to those who call evil good and good evil" (Isaiah 5:20). God is saying, *How could you believe what is bad is good and what is good is bad? I'm against it, because it's going to cause you so much pain.*

Don't buy into the lie that if an image makes something look good, it actually *is* good. Magazine images of anorexic girls are *not* good. Articles telling young women how to have sex with a "partner" and not a husband are *not* good. The devil is a liar, remember? He masquerades as an angel of light, presenting himself as a messenger of the good, when underneath the façade he is after your soul. If he can get you to believe his lies, he can have you—and that's what he wants!

God's girls must practice distinguishing truth from lies. When you flip through magazines or check out images on social media, see if you can discern God's beautiful truth from the devil's lies.

Satan himself masquerades as an angel of light.

2 Corinthians 11:14

Day 17

Your Beauty

Jewel for Your Journey

Let the king be enthralled by your beauty;
honor him, for he is your lord.

PSALM 45:11

This verse would make a great magazine headline, but you won't see it in *Cosmo*, *Glamour*, or *Allure*. Instead, you'll see 365 tips on how to "be beautiful." In the Bible, there are wonderful beauty tips, but they all have to do with your heart. Most of them pertain to the words you use and the way you treat people. First Peter 3:3-5 says your beauty comes from the inner self, the gentle and quiet spirit that is so persuasive you can win a man's heart without words.

The "gentle and quiet spirit" is Christ in you. You don't have to be a quiet personality to be beautiful to him. You can be expressive, emotional, and messed up! The women who came falling at Jesus's feet in the Gospels were passionate and unreserved. But he called them beautiful because their passion was a reflection of his heart.

The media doesn't define beauty as respect, gentleness, wisdom, discernment, and faith. But God is your Father, your Maker, and that is exactly how he defines beauty.

The question for you is whether you will go the way of the world or the way of the Word. Will you honor Christ as your king? Will you trust God enough to commit your body as a sacrifice to him? Will you honor your future husband now? Will your lips bring praise or cursing? Who will you be? Which way will you choose?

When you honor the king with your body, mind, heart, and soul, he looks upon you and is enthralled with your beauty. You have won his heart. And that lasts forever.

*Charm is deceptive, and beauty is fleeing; but a
woman who fears the LORD is to be praised.*

PROVERBS 31:30

Day 18

The Temple of You

Jewel for Your Journey

*Touch no unclean thing! Come out from it and be
pure, you who carry the articles of the LORD's house.*

ISAIAH 52:11

It used to be that people had to purify themselves from sin through sacrifice and cleansing. But when Jesus died he accomplished all that in one task, so that you can enter God's presence through faith.

When I first became a Christian, I didn't give up all my old ways immediately. I didn't suddenly become "perfect," and I still am not. But sin quickly became uncomfortable for me. Unhealthy relationships and habits convicted my spirit. I *knew* these things were out of line with God's will for me.

I rid myself of those things and allowed my relationship with Christ to fill me. The more time I spent in fellowship, the Word, and taking long walks with Jesus, the more I didn't long for those things of the world. Instead, I longed for him.

Being pure is a choice. Yes, Christ's sacrifice purifies us of sin, but choosing to live like a daughter of God, the temple of God, means making distinct choices to stay pure. For example, my husband and I chose not to live together before marriage. When we found ourselves tempted too often, we chose to not go beyond the goodnight kiss. He also chose an accountability partner who helped him stay pure. I know women who chose not to drink and not to be out of the public eye with a man, and who married as virgins. Those choices didn't happen by accident. They were purposeful decisions that helped them be victorious.

Do you have some choices you need to make? Are you allowing sin in your temple? What do you need to do to protect your heart, mind, and body so that they are clean houses for God's spirit to dwell? Spend time alone with God on these questions. Ask him if there is a lifestyle choice you need to make to preserve your purity. Being pure of mind, heart, and body is pleasing to him—because he lives in the temple of you.

> *Don't you know that you yourselves are God's temple*
> *and that God's Spirit dwells in your midst?*
>
> 1 CORINTHIANS 3:16

Forgive

Jewel for Your Journey

If you forgive other people when they sin against you, your heavenly Father will also forgive you. But if you do not forgive others their sins, your Father will not forgive your sins.

Matthew 6:14-15

When I burned the unsavory photos from my life as a model, I was purging myself of the bitterness I had towards the men in the modeling industry. Over a period of years, I also grappled with other people who had hurt me and the ways I had hurt myself. One by one and instance by instance, I forgave them all.

Sometimes it's easier to deal with outward sin than inward sin. Once we have turned away from sexual sin, we then deal with our hearts. Once we stop abusing our bodies, we then deal with our souls. Just as God delivers us from addiction, he also sees the deepest areas of our hearts that need mending. He sees what no one else sees.

In Deuteronomy 13–24, God repeatedly told his people to "purge the evil from among you." Why? Because he dwelled among them, and he is so good that evil cannot exist in his presence.

When we hold on to jealousy, bitterness, or rage, we are just as steeped in sin as when we sin outwardly. God's heart for you is to be clean in every way. That's why he is so serious about forgiveness. When Jesus died on the cross, the entire purpose was to offer free forgiveness for all men. So when we refuse to forgive, we stop up the flow of grace in our lives. If we do not forgive others, we will not be forgiven.

There was a time in my journey when I felt totally justified in my judgment of someone. I felt he had wronged me. But one day I was called to court for a series of traffic tickets, and as I waited for the judge, I thought about standing in front of God with my offender. I realized I couldn't judge his sin when mine had been forgiven.

I decided to release my offender. And when I approached the judge, he freely granted me mercy, which I did not deserve.

Forgiveness is not easy, but it's a choice you make for your soul.

Take your offenders to the cross. Forgive the big stuff. Deal with it. Purge it. Then forgive little offenses quickly. As you have been shown mercy, be merciful. Your Father sees your extension of forgiveness as beautiful because it is a picture of his love in action.

> *I tell you, her many sins have been forgiven.*
>
> LUKE 7:47

Holy

Jewel for Your Journey

*Be holy because I, the L*ORD *your God, am holy.*

LEVITICUS 19:2

We always find out who we are in the reflection of who God is. He is the Father; we are his daughters. He is the Creator; we are his creations. He is holy; so are we. For him to be the Lord of the temples of us, we have to take a look at what "holiness" is.

In Romans 12:1-2, Paul urges us to offer our bodies "as a living sacrifice, holy and pleasing to God"—for this, he says, is our spiritual act of worship. "Do not conform any longer to the pattern of this world, but be transformed by the renewing of your mind," he writes. Certainly the pattern of this world does not tell women they are holy! Prostitution, sexting, drugs, abortion—they all portray the message that women are not holy and neither are their wombs.

But God begs to differ. He says you are a reflection of a holy God. Does that mean you have to be perfect? No. Jesus took all the repercussions of our imperfections on the cross. He died for our weaknesses.

But it does mean that you hold yourself to a higher standard. You are the one who declares: *My body is holy ground. The floor of my temple is inlaid with pure gold. I will wait for my husband on my wedding day. I am the Temple of the Lord Jesus Christ, and no one is going to mess with me!*

There is something so powerful about a woman who knows who she is. She attracts godly people because she has already decided to be godly. She is beautiful because she doesn't get her notions of beauty from the pattern of the world. She knows what a lie is, and she beholds the truth. She has set herself apart as holy ground.

Are you that girl? I understand what it is like to walk in sin and feel like I will never be free from its grasp. I also understand what it is to confess, lay that sin at his feet, and repent, choosing to live like I am holy.

Ask his Spirit to give you self-control, to reign in you, and to help you resist the sin that so easily entangles. Make a decision today to be holy, and trust the Holy Spirit to help you.

Do not conform to the pattern of this world, but be transformed by the renewing of your mind.

Romans 12:2

Inside Out

Jewel for Your Journey

*There he was transfigured before them. His face shone like
the sun, and his clothes became as white as the light.*

MATTHEW 17:2

Jesus had an inner circle. He didn't just blab his deepest secrets to
the masses. His most profound pain would be too overwhelming for everyone to know about. But he also knew the power of a tight-knit circle of friends.

Jesus spoke to the multitudes, teaching them with story and life-changing truth. He traveled with a company of at least 12 men, and probably as many women. Surely they saw the up-close and personal Jesus in a way the crowds never did. But when Jesus needed to meet with God, he went alone to pray. In some of his most intense moments, however, he asked his friends to accompany him.

In Matthew 17, Jesus takes Peter, James, and John up the mountain and we see the first small group at work. They meet up with Moses and Elijah, and there, with the six of them present, God speaks to them. The disciples don't understand what is happening. They are just along for the ride when Jesus turns himself inside out and blazing glory explodes from him. Right in front of their eyes, he transforms from a common-looking man to a blaze of light, bright as the sun. His clothes turn whiter than any bleach could make them.

Everyone needs a Moses and Elijah—a couple people who know you inside and out, who are further along in their journey, and with whom you can speak openly in private. And everyone should have a

Peter, James, and John—those who journey with you even when they don't know where you are going.

Jesus went unmasked. Not with everyone, but with a precious few. Who do you go unmasked with? Who knows your true self? Who are your Moses and Elijah? Your Peter, James, and John? Join with them regularly. Do not try to walk the road of Christ alone. You are meant to have companions on this journey. Choose your friends wisely. There will be times you will need them to laugh with you, cry with you, pray for you, and hold your hands high. Whenever you are together, God will be right there with you, and you will hear his voice.

> *For where two or three gather in my name, there am I with them.*
>
> MATTHEW 18:20

Day 22

Whitewashed Tombs

Jewel for Your Journey

Satan himself masquerades as an angel of light.

2 Corinthians 11:14

The heart of Jesus couldn't be more opposite that of the enemy. Jesus was humble, a man acquainted with rejection and familiar with suffering, yet his name is exalted above every name on earth.

God didn't exalt Jesus for his great looks or awesome talent. In fact, Isaiah 53:2-3 says he had nothing in his outward appearance to attract us to him. No beauty or majesty that we should desire him. He was "despised and rejected by mankind." But while man looks at the outward appearance, God sees the heart, and Jesus's heart was supremely beautiful.

Satan, on the other hand, looked good on the outside but was ugly within. Ezekiel 28:12 likens him to a "seal of perfection, full of wisdom and perfect in beauty," but his heart became proud on account of his beauty. He didn't want people to worship God. He wanted people to worship him.

God would have none of it. When God crushed the body of his Son on the cross, he crushed Satan's power forever; he has come to a horrible end and will be no more.

So when Jesus encountered religious people who masqueraded as righteous but whose hearts were rotten, he called them whitewashed tombs who look beautiful on the outside but on the inside are filled with death. Masquerades remind him of the original snake.

Making things look pretty on the outside may earn you the applause of the world, but God is looking at the heart. And whose applause matters more than God's anyway?

Is your heart pure towards him? Is your motivation to do good things so that you will look good and people will approve, or is your motivation to do good an extension of his goodness towards you?

Jesus was beautiful from the inside out. Blazing glory, cloaked in humility. Now that's gorgeous.

> *He had no beauty or majesty to attract us to him, nothing*
> *in his appearance that we should desire him...But he*
> *was pierced for our transgressions, he was crushed for*
> *our iniquities; the punishment that brought us peace*
> *was on him, and by his wounds we are healed.*
>
> ISAIAH 53:2,5

Day 23

Unmasked

Jewel for Your Journey

Whenever anyone turns to the Lord, the veil is taken away. Now the Lord is the Spirit, and where the Spirit of the Lord is, there is freedom.

2 Corinthians 3:16-17

One of the most harmful things we can do is mask our pain. Women and girls who stuff their hurtful experiences eventually turn on themselves or on others. It's not healthy to keep truths locked in the darkness.

For years after I left the modeling industry, I wrote about my experiences in creative writing classes, pretending they were fiction. I didn't want to use the word "I" as if *I* was the one in my story who was a mess. I wanted to make the girl in my story the hurting one.

When I finally admitted I was her, I had to grapple with the pain I had experienced. In 2 Corinthians 3, we read that when we go before the Lord, we can go unveiled, uncovered, unmasked. When we open our hearts bare before him, God's Spirit is with us, and we are free. Free to be a mess. Free to question. Free to be honest, real, and uncensored.

Whenever you turn to the Lord with your truth, faith in Christ tears the veil of separation between you and God. If we are willing to look at ourselves and confess what we want to change, and if we are willing to be honest about the hurt others have caused us and we have caused others, he transforms our experience into something to strengthen us. Jesus's compassion for us is great, and his mercy is unfathomable. He is quick to forgive and allows our suffering to be like sandpaper that polishes out the best in us.

The more you go unmasked before the Lord, the more you become like him. He literally changes you from the inside out, so that your heart reflects his heart.

Get honest. Get real. Get before him. And get ready to be changed!

> *You are a forgiving God, gracious and compassionate,*
> *slow to anger and abounding in love.*
>
> NEHEMIAH 9:17

Day 24

Shine

Jewel for Your Journey

You will shine among them like stars in the sky.

PHILIPPIANS 2:15

There is a special young woman in my life who is a budding star. She has incredible musical talent and went to the top of *American Idol*. It's been an exciting journey for her but a battle too. The world of Hollywood tugs on her to dress more scantily. "It would be so much easier, Jen," she tells me, "if I just dressed sexier." She's had opportunities to be a part of TV shows that promote homosexuality; she's been surrounded by people sleeping around and drinking; yet she won't compromise her faith in Christ or her values. I'm proud of her for being a true star by reflecting the love of Christ in a world that denies him.

What is God's definition of a star? Jesus is the Bright Morning Star, and true stars want to reflect him in all that we do. We have to decide if we are going to reflect the image of the world or his image in the world.

Did you know you and I are stars too? Daniel 12:3 says, "Those who are wise will shine like the brightness of the heavens, and those who lead many to righteousness, like the stars for ever and ever." That's eternal brightness, not just temporary stardom.

Do you want to shine? To be radiant? Beautiful? Keep yourself blameless, and hold out the word of life. Be wise. Make good choices when no one but God is looking. Be a leader, and lead others to righteousness. You will shine, and your light will last forever.

Those who look to him are radiant.

PSALM 34:5

Submit

Jewel for Your Journey

Submit to one another out of reverence for Christ.

EPHESIANS 5:21

I learned the hard way that complaining and arguing weren't pretty. I had a hard time submitting to my husband because I always thought I knew better. One day my mentor told me that I had a problem with submission because I had "an exalted view of my own wisdom." Ouch! She was right. I did. I always thought I knew more, and I was wrong. My life is much happier when I pray about things and honor my husband's role in my life. He and my mentors are my covering and I trust their voice, even when they tell me what's hard to hear.

It's easy to say your beauty does not come from outward appearance and that it is the inner self that makes you powerful. But 1 Peter 3:1-6 shows us that true beauty is about submission, honor, and respect.

Beauty is as beauty does. Despite the world's definition of stars—who more often than not dishonor themselves, their future husbands, and God—God's definition includes honoring your own body and honoring others.

Honoring the voice of your parents, mentors, teachers—whoever God has put as a covering over you—shows a submissive spirit. They may not always be right, but God will bless your heart for staying open to their wisdom and input in your life. Did you know that honoring your parents is the first commandment with a promise? "Honor your father and mother...so that it may go well with you and that you may enjoy long life on the earth." There is great blessing in honoring your covering.

Likewise, the holy women of the past made themselves beautiful by honoring their husbands. They won people by their pure behavior, not their words. When people see our submissive spirits, they are won over. They are drawn to our beauty, because it's real. It comes from the inside out.

Do you believe beauty comes from the inner self? Where in your spirit do you think the Lord wants to grow you in beauty? Do you argue against your covering, the people God has put over you? Is there an area you can grow? Ask the Lord to reveal these things to you so you can be all he's made you to be.

> *Your beauty should not come from outward adornment...*
> *Rather, it should be that of your inner self, the unfading*
> *beauty of a gentle and quiet spirit, which is of great worth*
> *in God's sight. For this is the way the holy women of the*
> *past who put their hope in God used to adorn themselves.*
>
> 1 PETER 3:3-5

The Lamp

Jewel for Your Journey

*You are the light of the world. A town built on a hill
cannot be hidden. Neither do people light a lamp and
put it under a bowl. Instead they put it on its stand,
and it gives light to everyone in the house. In the same
way, let your light shine before others, that they may see
your good deeds and glorify your Father in heaven.*

MATTHEW 5:14,16

Having a lit lamp makes a home feel warm and inviting. In our jewel for today, Jesus tells us we are the light of the world, and then he offers two pictures: a public light and a private light.

He describes us as a "town built on a hill." That's the public light. At school, church, or even at the grocery store, people will be drawn to the light of Christ in you. They will see something different about you, and hopefully what they see is extraordinary love. Healing. Hope. Faith. Kindness. Humility. Gentleness. Peace.

But we are not only a public light; we are also a private light. Jesus compares us to a lamp, which gives light to everyone in the house. He tells us not to put our lights under a bowl. *The Message* says, "You don't think I'm going to hide you under a bucket, do you? I'm putting you on a light stand…shine!"

Our family went through a few years of really tough trials. We experienced a lot of pain. There were many days in this season when I was an effective "town built on a hill" but not a very good "lamp" in my home. I could go out and share my heart and teach the Word and shine the light of Jesus—piece of cake! But then I would go home and put a bucket over my head and turn my light completely off. I was looking at our circumstance so much that I was reflecting it, and when we do that, joy is stolen from us. We are the lamp in our homes, and we give light to everyone in the house. We simply cannot decide life's too hard and throw a blanket over our light. We have to turn away from the circumstances and look up at Jesus.

Are you struggling with some circumstances beyond your control? Are there things in your life you wish you could change but you can't? Stop looking at your circumstances. Look at your God. Keep your eyes fixed on him. He will shine his heart back at you.

> *Keep your eyes on Jesus, who both began and finished this race we're in. Study how he did it. Because he never lost sight of where he was headed.*
>
> HEBREWS 12:1-3 MSG

The Thief

Jewel for Your Journey

The thief comes only to steal and kill and destroy; I have come that they may have life, and have it to the full.

John 10:10

Jesus says the devil is not only a snake, a liar, and a murderer, but he is a thief. His *only* purpose? To steal, kill, and destroy. Don't let that scare you. By the blood of Christ, you have dominion over him.

But you must be wary of his ways. He wants to steal. Steal your time, your focus, your energy, your influence. He wants to rob you of your value by getting you to compare yourself to others. Steal your innocence by sexualizing you before its time. Steal your future by getting you to follow his ways. He's a murderer! He wants to kill your spirit, destroy your future marriage, your ministry, and the profound value of your impact in the world. Why? Because you are made in the image of God, and he is dead mad at God. God kicked him out of heaven and won't ever let him back in. But you and I have entrance home through the blood.

As a young woman in the world, I want you to be wary of his tricks. I want you to know how he works to drown out the voice of God, get your focus on yourself, and draw you away from the development of your gifts and talents. And I want you to know that Jesus came to give you an abundant life—life to the full. He wants to give you all the desires of your heart, as long as they're in line with what is best for you. Trust him with your life.

What does life to the full look like for you? Can you taste it, see it, smell it? Where is Jesus in your life? Listen for his voice, teaching you how to drive your life like a vehicle that gets you to the destination of your heart's desires.

> *Take delight in the LORD, and he will*
> *give you the desires of your heart.*
>
> PSALM 37:4

Day 28

Face to Face

Jewel for Your Journey

Look at us!

ACTS 3:4

We love to be looked in the eye. Sometimes, however, the people who are sending us messages through their mouths and eyes are posting unkind notes on our hearts. Sometimes life gets hard and we want to disappear. People look past us, perhaps. No one notices. Or, even more painful, people stare or cut us down. Maybe we are looking for a place to fit; a place to shine; a place to find approval and affirmation and a place to belong.

I understand this need to be seen, heard, known, and loved. We all have this very legitimate, human need God put in our hearts. Yet sometimes we look to people to fill it, the mirror, the masks, the media. Sometimes we open our screens and peer in to see if someone notices us, if anyone agreed with our comment, liked our post, read our blog, watched our video, or bought our idea. Why do we do this? Because we all have a God-sized hole in our hearts. It's easier to look at the screen than it is to open our Bibles. *I have loved you with an everlasting love,* he says to us (Jeremiah 31:3). Yet when our eyes are fixed on the screen, searching for something we already have access to through his Holy Spirit, we can miss this love that changes us, heals us, and raises us to life.

In Acts 3:1-10, a beggar encountered Peter and John. He was lame from birth, and I believe his life was spent watching people rush past him or toss a few coins in his cup. I bet he felt invisible. Broken. Longing for something to fill him. When Peter and John came to the gate and saw him there, they looked straight at him and said to him, "Look at us!"

They were fully present, fully aware, and fully awake to the hurt in this man's face and body. They gave him Jesus, the one thing on the whole of the earth that would fill him and heal him. They reached out and touched him, and by a miracle his ankles grew strong and he was miraculously healed.

I used to be a little like the beggar, looking for something to fill my cup. Now I'm like Peter and John. I'm healed and I'm looking around for beggars. I hope I don't miss them because of the screens demanding my attention. I hope you don't either. Face to face is where the real stuff happens, the stuff that changes lives and heals hearts. Don't miss it.

Praise the Lord, my soul, and forget not all his benefits—
who forgives all your sins and heals all your diseases, who
redeems your life from the pit and crowns you with love
and compassion, who satisfies your desires with good
things so that your youth is renewed like the eagle's.

PSALM 103:2-5

Day 29

The Most High

Jewel for Your Journey

He will command his angels concerning
you to guard you in all your ways.

PSALM 91:10-11

Sometimes I get scared. I worry. I doubt. We can't ever see very far down the road ahead, and the fear of the unknown can wrestle us to the ground.

I had a dream once that something was trying to suffocate me, to stop my words and my breath—and it had me by the throat.

"Jesus…" I kept trying to say. "Jesus." But I couldn't get any sound out. I persisted until finally I spoke his name. The choking stopped.

His name has power, and at the name of Jesus, the demons flee. They know God's name, and they shudder at it. When we know who we are and whose we are, we have no reason to fear. He will give us the words to say. He will rescue us. He will provide for us. He will take care of us. He will never leave us or turn his back on us.

His love is unfailing. He loves us with an everlasting love. "Though the mountains be shaken and the hills be removed, yet my unfailing love for you will not be shaken," says the Lord (Isaiah 54:10).

He says, *You are my beloved, precious chosen one, and I adore you. I picked you and you picked me. I used to live in temples built by human hands, but now I reside in you.*

The Most High, the King of Kings, the Great and Awesome God lives in you. So do not fear, my beloved.

I am with you always, even to the end of the age. I am the Alpha and the Omega, the beginning and the end, and I hold you with my righteous right hand. You will never fall from my palm. I will always catch you, and I never miss.

> *Whoever dwells in the shelter of the Most High*
> *will rest in the shadow of the Almighty.*
>
> PSALM 91:1

Redeemed

Jewel for Your Journey

*Listen, I tell you a mystery: We will not all
sleep, but we will all be changed—in a flash, in
the twinkling of an eye, at the last trumpet.*

1 Corinthians 15:51-52

When I had my dream of heaven, I saw several things: Jesus, robust and wonderful; an amazing temple where he is the lamp; a fun, cuddly sleepover where Jesus read us a story; a vast, grand, and beautiful meadow; my husband, young, strong and completely redeemed, and our whole family walking through the meadow together with our dogs.

Throughout the entire experience, I felt the fullness of joy. It was abundant and overflowing. It was bliss. Profound satisfaction. There was no pain, no striving for things to be different. Only joy in all its fullness.

When Jesus describes himself as the bread and water of life and promises us life to the full, he means it. When he comes back for us, we'll know it's him. He'll come riding on a white horse, the armies of heaven following him. He'll come take back his church, his bride—you and me and all believers.

In a flash, in the twinkling of an eye, we will be transformed. Redeemed.

Redeemed, he will make all things new.

Redeemed, all things will be made whole.

Redeemed, it will be more beautiful than you know. There will be no flaw, no frailty, no failure. Only the fullness of joy.

See you there!

Your eyes will see the king in his beauty
and view a land that stretches afar.

Isaiah 33:17

About the Author

Jennifer Strickland is wife to her best friend, Shane. Together they have three beautiful children, Olivia, Zachary, and Samuel. They live in North Texas, where they enjoy the Legacy8 family ranch. Their family's hope is also to build a restoration house where young women and girls can be healed. Their ministry, U R More, is devoted to changing the world one heart at a time. To watch video vignettes, post a book review, or learn more about Jennifer's powerful resources and live events, visit www.jenniferstrickland.net.

To learn more about Jennifer Strickland or to read sample chapters, visit www.harvesthousepublishers.com